TRIANGLE-FREE QUILTS

TRIANGLE-FREE QUILTS

— JUDY HOPKINS —

Martingale™
& COMPANY

Dedication

FOR GEORGE TAYLOR, a terrific technician, willing collaborator, and loyal friend.

Acknowledgments

SPECIAL THANKS, as always, to the quiltmakers and collectors, the hand and machine quilters, and the pattern testers: Becky Crook, Judy DeLano, Barbara Ford, Judy Forrest, Maggie French, Julie Fugate, Peter Hale, Michele Hall, Julie Kimberlin, Ann Liburd, Anne Richardson, Jeanie Smith, George Taylor, and Tina Tomsen. Thanks also to Marsha McCloskey and Clothworks/Fasco Fabric Sales Co., Inc., for the Staples samples used in "Arctic Nights," and to Sharon Risedorph for photographing "Maggie's Quilt."

Martingale™
& COMPANY

That Patchwork Place®

That Patchwork Place® is an imprint of Martingale & Company™.

Triangle-Free Quilts
© 2002 by Judy Hopkins

Martingale & Company
20205 144th Avenue NE
Woodinville, WA 98072-8478 USA
www.martingale-pub.com

Printed in Hong Kong
08 07 06 05 04 03 02   10 9 8 7 6 5 4 3 2 1

Library of Congress Cataloging-in-Publication Data

Hopkins, Judy
  Triangle-free quilts / Judy Hopkins.
    p. cm.
  ISBN 1-56477-393-0
  1. Patchwork—Patterns. 2. Quilting—Patterns. I. Title.
  TT835 .H576 2002
  746.46'041—dc21
                                        2002011799

Credits

PRESIDENT	*Nancy J. Martin*
CEO	*Daniel J. Martin*
PUBLISHER	*Jane Hamada*
EDITORIAL DIRECTOR	*Mary V. Green*
MANAGING EDITOR	*Tina Cook*
TECHNICAL EDITOR	*Laurie Baker*
COPY EDITOR	*Liz McGehee*
DESIGN DIRECTOR	*Stan Green*
ILLUSTRATOR	*Laurel Strand*
COVER AND TEXT DESIGNER	*Trina Stahl*
PHOTOGRAPHER	*Brent Kane*

Mission Statement

We are dedicated to providing quality products and service by working together to inspire creativity and to enrich the lives we touch.

CONTENTS

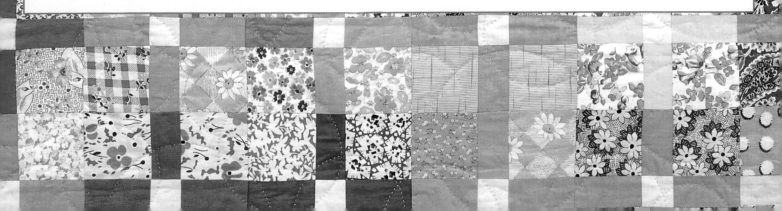

INTRODUCTION

ODAY'S BUSY QUILTERS look for patterns that can be made quickly and that result in pleasing quilts; many deliberately avoid designs that include triangles. This book was created especially for all those devoted fans of squares, rectangles, and strips. It features a classy collection of quilts made with simple shapes and speedy cutting and construction techniques. And they're all absolutely, positively, completely triangle-free!

Some of the projects are based on well-known traditional blocks and classic settings; in others, familiar elements are combined in unusual ways. Many of the quilts rely on interesting, beautiful fabrics for their appeal. The flag quilt "United We Stand" (page 30) has a little appliqué. None of the other projects have appliqué elements, so I hadn't planned to include this quilt in the book, but after 9/11, it seemed a good thing to do.

There's something for everyone here, from big bold blocks to pleasant pastel parfaits. I know you'll enjoy making these easy, eye-catching quilts.

Judy Hopkins

COLOR RUNS

WHEN YOU MAKE a quilt from a pattern book like this one, where the quilt's size, setting arrangement, and color scheme are specified, it's the fabrics you choose to work with that make your project personal and unique. Many of the quilts in this book are multifabric quilts that rely on runs of fabric in particular color families. The materials list, for example, might call for eight assorted cream prints and eight assorted dark green prints. Choose prints in a variety of scales and visual textures, and try not to overmatch the colors. Don't hesitate to include two-color and multicolor prints in your color runs; they often add needed liveliness to a quilt.

For the cream prints, you could choose eight different prints in light, creamy colors that range from ivory to ecru.

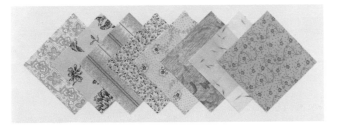

A Cream Color Run

A color run in the green family might include forest greens, moss greens, emerald greens, and blue-greens. Spice up the mix by adding a small amount of an adjacent color, such as blue, and/or a neutral, such as brown or black. Neutrals can be added to any color scheme without changing it; they add interest without calling attention to themselves.

A Green Color Run

If you're working entirely from scraps or from yardage on hand and don't have enough fabrics in a particular color family, just use assorted colors of the same or similar value. A run of darks, for instance, could include greens, browns, purples, navy blues, deep reds, and blacks.

Yardage Requirements

THE YARDAGE REQUIREMENTS for the quilt patterns that start on page 30 are based on fabric that is at least 42" wide after preshrinking. If your fabric is narrower than 42", you may need additional fabric.

Some of the materials lists specify fat quarters. A standard quarter yard is cut selvage to selvage and measures 9" by about 42". A fat quarter is a piece of fabric 18" by about 21". Most quilt shops offer precut fat quarters; some will cut fat quarters from the bolt on request.

All the quilts in this book have borders with straight-cut corners, with the exception of "Patch Patch Patch," which uses borders with corner squares (see "Adding Borders" on pages 18–19). For both border types, strips are cut along the crosswise grain (selvage to selvage) and seamed

where extra length is needed, unless otherwise specified in the project instructions. Purchase additional fabric if you want mitered corners or borders cut along the lengthwise grain.

Yardage requirements for backings are calculated to use the least amount of fabric. For the quilts in this book, you'll cut two or three lengths of fabric from the specified yardage and join them along the long edges using a ½" seam. The pattern instructions will tell you whether the backing seams are intended to be oriented crosswise or lengthwise in the quilt (see "Preparing the Backing and Batting" on pages 20–21).

For bindings, yardage requirements assume ⅜"-wide (finished), double-fold binding, made from straight-grain strips cut 2½" wide (see "Binding" on pages 26–28).

FABRIC CONTENT AND PREPARATION

Most quilters prefer working with good-quality, 100% cotton fabrics, but it's not always possible to observe the "100% cotton rule" with quilts created from scraps or from fabric collections of long standing. While polyester content can make small patchwork pieces difficult to cut and sew accurately, I cheerfully include fabrics of uncertain content from my collection when the color or pattern seems appropriate for a particular quilt. Occasionally I'll even buy a blend, if it has unique potential.

Wash all fabrics to preshrink, test for color-fastness, and eliminate excess dye. To preserve the sizing and keep the fabric from raveling, place the fabric in a sink or washing machine with tepid water and soak for ten minutes; don't use soap or agitate. Run the washing machine through the spin cycle or gently hand-wring the fabric to remove excess water. Dry in a dryer, using a warm to hot setting. Put a large, heavy towel in the dryer with the fabric to reduce twisting and tangling. I wash fabrics as soon as I bring them home from the store and smooth and fold them as they come out of the dryer, pressing only those pieces that are impossibly wrinkled.

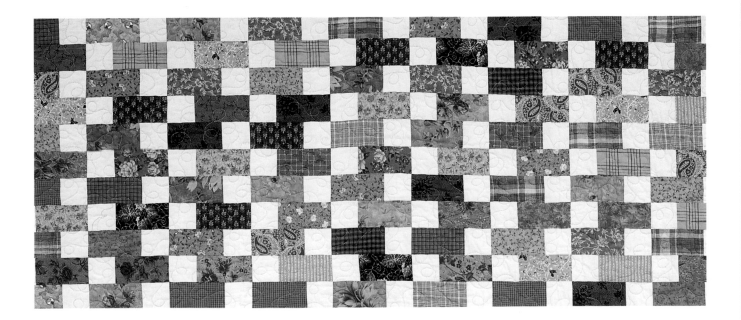

ROTARY CUTTING

THE TRIANGLE-FREE quilts in this book are all rotary cut. You'll be cutting strips from fabric and cutting squares and rectangles from some of those strips. Other strips may be joined to make strip units, which are then cut into segments.

All cutting measurements given in the pattern instructions include ¼"-wide seam allowances; don't add seam allowances to the dimensions given.

Rotary-cutting and strip-piecing techniques sometimes yield more pieces than actually are needed to make a particular block or quilt. For example, cutting all the way to the end of a strip unit without counting the number of pieces cut may give you more pieces than you need. Use any leftovers as part of a pieced back, or toss them into the scrap bag for a future quilt.

Equipment

BASIC ROTARY-CUTTING tools include a medium-size (45 mm) rotary cutter and an 18" x 24" self-healing cutting mat. You'll also need a 24"-long acrylic cutting ruler and a 6" or 8" cutting square, both marked in ⅛" increments. Smaller cutting mats and rulers in other sizes can be useful but aren't required for the projects in this book.

When a rotary blade seems dull, take your rotary cutter apart and put a small drop of sewing-machine oil on the blade; wipe both sides carefully with a soft, clean cloth. Wipe the safety guard and other parts before you reassemble the cutter. If the blade still isn't cutting cleanly through the fabric, replace it.

Keep your cutter's safety guard closed except when you're actually making a cut. Never leave a rotary cutter, open or closed, within reach of children! Dispose of used blades safely.

Cutting Strips, Squares, and Rectangles

THE FIRST STEP in most rotary-cutting operations is to straighten the raw edge of the fabric. Fold the fabric in half lengthwise, aligning the selvages. Lay the fabric on the cutting mat with the fold of the fabric closest to you and the bulk of the fabric to your left. Reverse the layout if you're left-handed.

Align a horizontal line of the long ruler with the fold of the fabric. Cut along the edge of the ruler, through both layers of fabric. Always roll the cutter away from your body. Hold the ruler firmly

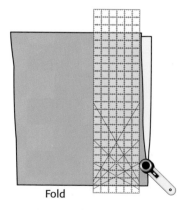

Fold

in place as you cut, keeping your fingers well away from the sharp rotary blade. Start rolling the cutter before you reach the fabric edge and continue across the fabric, using firm, even pressure and keeping the blade pressed against the ruler as you go.

Close the safety guard on the rotary cutter immediately after making the cut. Make sure you've cut through all the fabric layers before you lift the ruler.

Move to the opposite side of the table, or rotate the cutting mat so that the bulk of the fabric is to your right. If necessary, accordion-fold the fabric and pile it on the mat, being careful not to disturb your freshly cut edge.

Cut strips to the width given in the pattern instructions, measuring from the straight cut on the left. If you need a 3" wide strip, for example, place the 3" line of the ruler on the straightened edge of the fabric. Combine your cutting square with the long ruler to make cuts wider than the long ruler allows.

Fold

Open and check the strips occasionally to make sure your cuts are straight. If the strips develop a "bend" in the middle (a fairly common occurrence), restraighten the edge of the fabric before you proceed.

To cut squares and rectangles from strips, straighten the selvage ends of the folded strip by aligning a horizontal line of the cutting square with the long edge of the folded strip. Cut along the edge of the ruler through both layers, removing the selvages in the process. Rotate the mat so

that the clean-cut end of the strip is on the left. Align the proper measurement on your cutting square with the straightened end of the strip, and cut the fabric into squares or rectangles the width of the strip. Sometimes you can get an additional piece by unfolding the strip when you reach the right-hand edge.

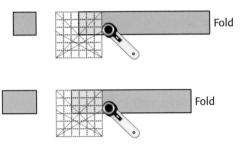

Fold

Fold

Making and Cutting Strip Units

FOR MANY OF the quilts in this book, you'll be making blocks and units by cutting strips of fabric, sewing the strips together in a specific order to make strip units, and then cutting the strip units into segments.

1. Make the strip units and press the seams as described in the pattern. Press from the right side first, then turn the units over and press from the wrong side to be sure that all the seam allowances face the proper direction. Press carefully to avoid stretching.

2. Straighten the right end of each strip unit by aligning a horizontal line of the cutting square with one of the strip unit's internal seams and cutting along the edge of the ruler. Place the straightened end on the left, align the desired measurement on your cutting square with the straightened end, and cut.

MACHINE PIECING

A WELL-MAINTAINED STRAIGHT-STITCH sewing machine is adequate for most quilt-making operations. If you're using a zigzag sewing machine, replace the zigzag throat plate with a plate that has a small round hole for the needle to pass through, one especially designed for straight stitching. Clean and oil your machine frequently.

Use sewing-machine needles properly sized for cotton fabrics and change them often; dull or bent needles can snag your fabric and can cause your machine to skip stitches. Set the stitch length at 10 to 12 stitches per inch. Make sure the tension is adjusted properly to produce smooth, even seams. Use 100% cotton thread; I use a medium greenish gray thread (the color you get when you mix all the Easter-egg dyes together) for piecing all but the lightest and darkest fabrics.

The most important skill for a quilter to master is sewing accurate ¼" seams. If your seam allowance is off by even a few threads, your seams may not match and your blocks may not be the desired finished size, which in turn will affect the measurements for everything else in the quilt.

Test your seam width by cutting three short strips of fabric, each exactly 2" wide. Join the pieces into a strip unit, press the seams, and measure the finished width of the center strip. If you're sewing an accurate ¼" seam, the center strip will measure exactly 1½". If it doesn't, you need to adjust or compensate for whatever you're using as a seam guide, whether it's a special ¼" sewing-machine foot, a particular needle-position setting,

an engraved line on your sewing machine, or simply a piece of tape you've put on your sewing-machine bed. Some quilters find they need to sew a scant ¼"—just a thread or two short of a full ¼"—to allow for take-up when seams are pressed.

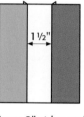

Seam 2" strips and measure the center.

If your seam-width test indicates you need a seam guide other than the edge of your presser foot or a line engraved on your machine, put a strip of moleskin or several layers of masking tape along your perfect ¼" line. Make sure the tape doesn't interfere with the feed dogs.

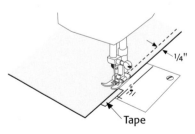

Tape

Use a hot iron on the cotton setting to gently press every seam before attaching a new piece of fabric. Some quilters use a dry iron, while others prefer steam.

I press seams open to make it easier to hand stitch the allover quilting patterns I commonly use for my quilts. However, the traditional quilters' rule is to press seams to one side, toward the darker fabric or toward the section with fewer seams. Side-pressed seams are stronger, and it's easier for most people to make corners meet properly when they can match opposing seams.

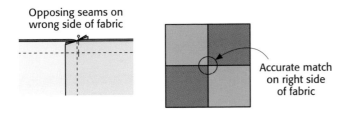

Opposing seams on wrong side of fabric

Accurate match on right side of fabric

Snip or pull out loose threads that have been caught in the seams as you press; it's easier to tidy up the pieces when you're pressing the individual seams than to go back over the entire quilt later.

When sewing two pieces or units together, you may need to ease excess fabric. One piece may be slightly longer than the other due to cutting discrepancies, seam-width variations, or simply because one fabric may behave differently than another. To ease, pin the pieces together at the seams and ends—and in between, if necessary—to distribute excess fabric. When you stitch the seam, place the shorter piece on top. The feed dogs will help ease the fullness of the longer piece.

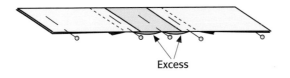

Excess

Save time and thread by chain piecing. Place the pieces that are to be joined right sides together with raw edges even; pin as necessary. When possible, arrange opposing seams so the top seam allowance faces toward the needle and the lower seam allowance faces toward you. Feed the units under the presser foot one after the other, without lifting the presser foot or clipping the connecting threads; backstitching isn't necessary. Clip the threads between the pieces either before or after pressing.

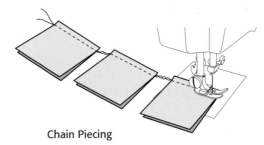

Chain Piecing

It's wise to sew a complete block together before you start working in this assembly-line fashion, to ensure that the pieces have been accurately cut and to identify piecing quirks you may need to watch out for.

Use a seam ripper to remove unwanted stitching. To avoid stretching the fabric, cut the thread every four or five stitches on one side of the fabric. Pull the thread on the reverse side; it should come out easily.

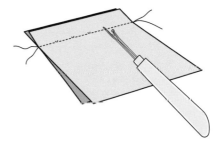

APPLIQUÉ

THE APPLIQUÉD STARS on "United We Stand" (page 30) were made with the freezer-paper method described below. Freezer paper has a plastic coating on one side; you can fold the seam allowances over the freezer-paper edges and iron them to the plastic-coated side to make perfectly shaped appliqués with smooth edges.

1. Make a template from stiff plastic or cardboard. *Do not add seam allowances to the template.* Trace around the template on the uncoated side of a piece of freezer paper.

2. Cut out the freezer-paper shape on the pencil line. *Do not add seam allowances.* Pin the freezer-paper shape, plastic-coated side up, to the wrong side of the fabric. Cut the appliqué shape from the fabric, adding ¼"-wide seam allowances around the outside edges of the freezer paper.

Wrong side of fabric

Add ¼" seam allowance all around.

3. Using a hot, dry iron, carefully turn and press the seam allowance over the freezer-paper edges, easing in any excess fabric. Clip inside points and fold outside points.

Press seam allowance over
freezer-paper edges.

4. Iron the design in place on the background fabric and appliqué the shape to the background, using thread that matches the appliqué piece. Catch just a few threads at the edge of the appliqué piece. Only a tiny stitch should show on the front of the quilt; the "traveling" is done on the back side.

Appliqué Stitch

5. After you've appliquéd the design, cut a small slit in the background fabric behind the appliqué. Cut away the background fabric, leaving a ¼"-wide seam allowance all around, and carefully remove the freezer paper.

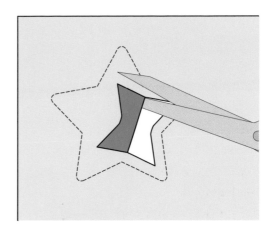

Leave ¼" seam allowance all around.

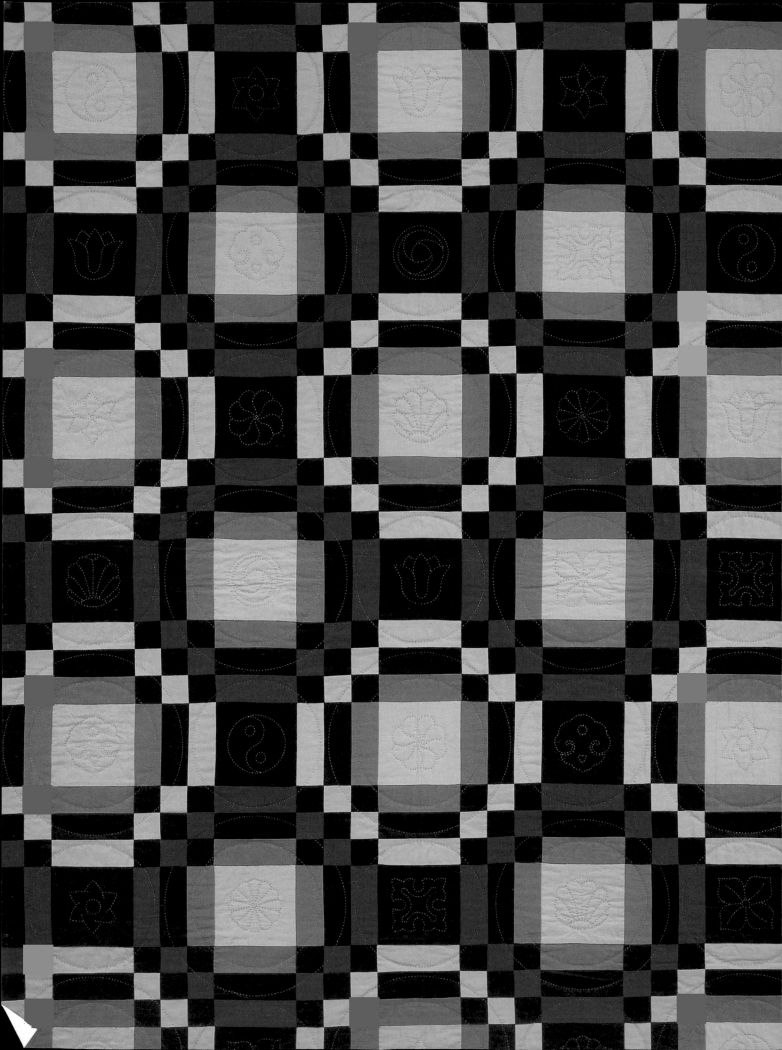

FINISHING YOUR QUILT

THIS SECTION BEGINS with basic information on squaring up blocks and setting them together and continues with instructions for other techniques you'll need to finish your quilt: adding borders, marking the quilting lines, preparing the backing and batting, layering the quilt, quilting or tacking, adding a hanging sleeve, binding, and making labels.

Squaring Up Blocks

IF YOUR blocks become distorted during the stitching process, square them up with a freezer-paper guide. Use an accurate cutting square and a pencil or permanent pen to draw a square (finished block size plus seam allowance) on the plain side of the freezer paper. Iron the freezer paper to your ironing-board cover, plastic-coated side down. Align the block edges with the penciled lines and pin the block in place. Gently steam-press. Let each block cool before you unpin it from the freezer-paper guide.

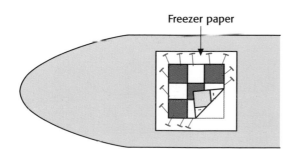

Freezer paper

Setting the Blocks Together

Straight Sets

The triangle-free quilts in this book are all straight-set quilts; the blocks and units are laid out with their edges parallel to the edges of the quilt. Constructing a straight-set quilt is simple and straightforward. When you set blocks side by side without sashing, simply stitch them together in horizontal rows, pressing the seams in opposite directions from row to row. Sew the rows together to complete the patterned section of the quilt, matching the seams between the blocks.

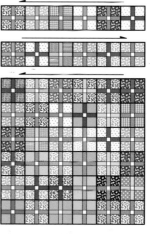

Straight-Set Quilt

If the pattern calls for alternate blocks, lay out the primary and alternate blocks in checkerboard fashion and stitch them together in rows, as shown above.

Straight Sets with Pieced Sashing

When setting blocks together with sashing pieces and sashing squares (corner squares cut from a different fabric), join the vertical sashing pieces to the blocks to form rows, beginning and ending each row with a sashing piece. Press seams toward the sashing pieces. Join the sashing squares to the horizontal sashing pieces to make pieced sashing strips, beginning and ending each row with a sashing square. Press seams toward the sashing pieces. Join the rows of blocks and the pieced sashing strips.

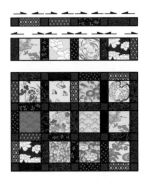

Straight-Set Quilt
with Pieced Sashing

Bar Quilts

In a bar quilt, various units are joined into rows, or bars, instead of blocks; the pattern emerges only after the bars are stitched together. Several different bar formats might be combined to form the overall pattern. Make sure the design, fabrics, and colors will come out as you intended by laying out the pieced units for several bars—or for the entire quilt—before you begin to sew.

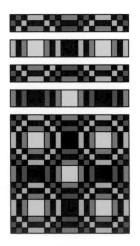

Adding Borders

BECAUSE EXTRA yardage is needed to cut borders on the lengthwise grain, borders for the quilts in this book are cut selvage to selvage and seamed as necessary to make strips long enough to border the quilt, unless otherwise specified in the cutting instructions. Remove the selvages and press the seams open for minimum visibility.

To ensure a flat, straight quilt, always take the border measurements across the center of the patterned section of the quilt, as described more fully below. This guarantees that the borders are of equal lengths on opposing sides of the quilt and brings the outer edges in line with the center dimension if discrepancies exist. Differences between the cut border strips and the outer edges of the quilt can be eased when the borders are joined to the quilt.

Borders with Straight-Cut Corners

1. Seam selvage-to-selvage strips along the short ends as necessary to make strips long enough to border the quilt; press the seams open.

2. Measure the length of the quilt through the center, from raw edge to raw edge. Cut two border strips to this measurement and join them to the sides of the quilt with a ¼" seam, matching the ends and centers and easing the edges to fit. Press the seams toward the borders.

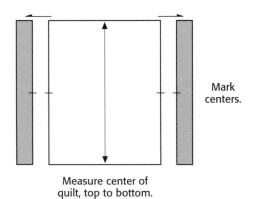

Mark
centers.

Measure center of
quilt, top to bottom.

3. Measure the width of the quilt at the center, including the border pieces you just added. Cut the remaining two border strips to this measurement and join them to the top and bottom edges of the quilt, matching ends and centers and easing as necessary. Press the seams toward the borders.

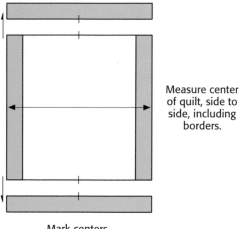

Measure center of quilt, side to side, including borders.

Mark centers.

Borders with Corner Squares

1. Seam selvage-to-selvage strips along the short ends as necessary to make strips long enough to border the quilt; press the seams open.

2. Measure the length and the width of the quilt at the center, from raw edge to raw edge. Cut two border strips to the lengthwise measurement and join them to the sides of the quilt with a ¼"-wide seam, matching the ends and centers and easing the edges to fit. Press the seams toward the borders.

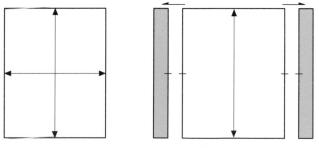

Mark centers.

3. Cut the remaining two border strips to the original crosswise measurement. Join plain or pieced corner squares to the ends of the border strips. The corner squares should be the same size as the width of the border strips. For example, if you cut your border strips 3" wide, your corner squares would need to be 3" square (raw edge to raw edge). Press the seams toward the border strips.

Stitch these units to the top and bottom edges of the quilt, matching ends, seams, and centers and easing as necessary. Press the seams toward the borders.

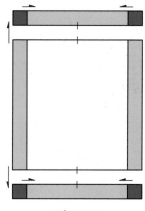

Mark centers.

Marking the Quilting Lines

BEFORE YOU mark the quilting lines, decide how much quilting is needed. The amount of quilting should be similar across the entire quilt. Fairly close, uniform quilting will help prevent sagging and distortion and will reduce stress on the fabric, batting, and quilting thread. With most battings, a 3" to 4" square is the largest area that can be left unquilted; check the manufacturer's instructions.

Marking may not be necessary if you're planning to quilt "in the ditch" (as close as possible to side-pressed seams), outline-quilt a uniform distance from the seams, or free-motion quilt in a random pattern. Some quiltmakers do outline quilting "by eye," though many others use ¼"-wide masking tape to mark these lines as they stitch.

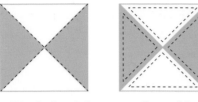

Quilting in the Ditch   Outline Quilting

You can use masking tape to mark any straight-line quilting design, or you can cut simple shapes from paper-backed self-adhesive plastic. Apply the tape or adhesive shape when you're ready to quilt and remove it promptly after you've quilted along its edge; adhesives left on the quilt too long may leave a residue that's difficult to remove. Lengths of tape and adhesive shapes can be reused several times.

Mark more complex quilting designs on the quilt top before layering it with batting and backing. A gridded transparent ruler is useful for measuring and marking straight lines and filler grids. If the fabrics are fairly light, you can place quilting patterns from books or magazines (or hand-drawn designs) underneath the quilt and trace directly onto the quilt. Use a light table or put your work against a window if you have trouble seeing the design.

If you can't see through the quilt fabric, mark the design directly onto the quilt top. Use a precut plastic quilting stencil or make your own by drawing or tracing a design onto clear plastic; cut out the lines with a double-bladed craft knife, leaving "bridges" every inch or two so the stencil will hold its shape. You also can trace the design onto plain paper (or make a photocopy); cover the paper with one or two layers of clear, self-adhesive plastic; and cut out the lines. Put small pieces of double-stick tape on the back of the stencil to keep it in place as you mark the quilting lines.

If you're using an allover quilting pattern that doesn't relate directly to the seams or to a design element of the quilt, you may find it easier to mark the quilting lines on the backing fabric and quilt from the back. Or, use a medium- to large-scale print for the backing and simply quilt around the motifs that appear in the print.

When marking quilting lines, work on a hard, smooth surface. Lines drawn with a Berol Non-Photo Blue pencil will show up on both light and dark fabrics. The marks will generally remain through the quilting process but will wash out once the quilting is completed.

Preparing the Backing and Batting

THE QUILT backing should be at least 6" wider and 6" longer than the quilt top. Some quilters buy extra-wide cotton to use for backing, but most simply use standard-width yardage and seam two or three lengths together to make a backing of adequate size.

In this book, fabric requirements for backings are calculated to use the least amount of yardage; you'll cut lengths of fabric and join them along the long edges with a ½" seam. Trim off selvages before you stitch; press backing seams open if you plan to hand quilt.

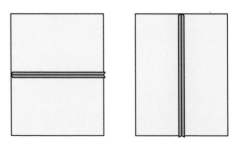

The pattern instructions will tell you whether the backing seams are intended to be oriented crosswise or lengthwise in the quilt.

For more variety, or simply to be more frugal, piece a multifabric backing. Use fabric and blocks left over from piecing the front of the quilt; add other fabrics and leftovers from your stash. Quilters have even been known to use quilt tops they're not particularly proud of to back quilts they like better!

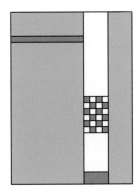

Batting comes packaged in standard bed sizes, or you can buy it by the yard. Several weights, or thicknesses, are available. Thick battings are fine for tied, tacked, or tufted quilts and comforters; choose a thinner batting if you intend to quilt by hand or machine.

Batting is available in 100% cotton; 100% polyester; and an 80% cotton, 20% polyester blend. The blend supposedly combines the best features of the two fibers. All-cotton batting is soft and drapable, but produces quilts that are rather flat. Many quilters like the antique look, but some find cotton batting difficult to hand quilt. Glazed or bonded polyester batting is sturdy, easy to quilt through, and requires less quilting than cotton. Polyester has more loft than cotton, but it can lose much of its bounce after repeated washings. Polyester fibers sometimes migrate through fabric, creating tiny white "beards" on the surface of a quilt.

Try a variety of different battings. Eventually you'll be able to judge which one is best for a particular project.

Unroll your batting and let it relax overnight before you layer your quilt, or put it in the dryer and air-dry it for about twenty minutes. Some battings may need to be prewashed, while others definitely should not be; be sure to check the manufacturer's instructions.

Layering and Basting the Quilt

ONCE YOU'VE marked your quilt top, pieced and pressed your backing, and let your batting relax, you're ready to layer and baste the quilt. Work on a large dining room table, a Ping-Pong table, or on several banquet tables pushed together. Sometimes you can arrange to use the tables at your quilt shop or church when they're not otherwise occupied.

1. Spread the backing on the table, wrong side up, and anchor it with masking tape or binder clips. Center the batting over the backing, smoothing out any wrinkles.

2. Center the quilt top on the batting, right side up; gently smooth any fullness to the sides and corners. Keep the major horizontal and vertical seams, such as those that attach the borders to the quilt, as straight as possible.

3. For hand quilting, baste the three layers together with a long needle and light-colored thread; start in the center and work diagonally

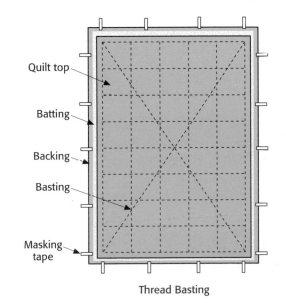

Thread Basting

to each corner, making a large X. Continue basting, laying in a grid of horizontal and vertical lines no more than 6" apart. Finish by basting around the outside edges.

For machine quilting, baste the layers with No. 2 rustproof safety pins placed 3" to 4" apart. Secure the outside edges with straight pins.

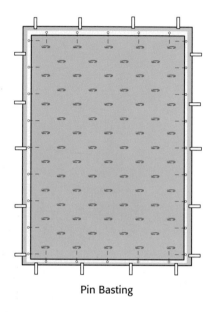

Pin Basting

A quilt-tack tool can be used to baste quilts for either hand or machine quilting. The method is fast and holds the layers securely. The T-shaped tabs of the tacks are easy to remove if they get in the way of the needle.

Quilt Tacks

Quilting

Machine Quilting

With machine quilting, you can quickly complete quilts that might otherwise languish on the shelf. It's helpful to have a large, flat work surface to support the quilt during the machine-quilting process.

Marking the quilting design isn't necessary if you plan to quilt in the ditch, outline-quilt a uniform distance from seam lines, or free-motion quilt in a random pattern. If you plan to follow a grid or use a complex pattern, mark the quilting lines before you layer the quilt.

For straight-line machine quilting and for large, easy curves, use a walking foot to help feed the quilt layers through the machine without shifting or puckering. Usually the walking foot (sometimes called an even-feed foot) is a separate attachment, although some sewing machines have a built-in dual-feed system that does the same job as a walking foot.

Walking Foot Attachment

Use free-motion quilting to outline-quilt a fabric motif or to do stippling or other intricate curved-line designs. When free-motion quilting, use a darning foot and lower the feed dogs of your sewing machine. Guide the fabric in the direction of the design as if the needle were a stationary pencil. Because the fabric moves freely, stitch length is determined by how fast you run the machine and how fast you feed the fabric under the foot. With practice, you'll soon get the feel of controlling the motion of the fabric with your hands. Running the machine fairly fast makes it easier to sew smooth lines.

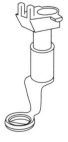

Darning Foot

Experiment with stars, scribbles, and gentle loops. Try to keep the spacing between quilting lines consistent over the entire project. Avoid leaving large blank spaces; with most battings, a 3" to 4" square is the largest area that can be left unquilted. Remove the safety pins as you quilt.

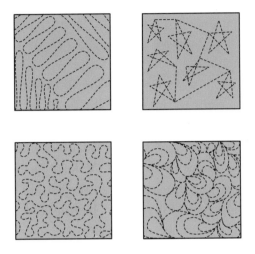

For comprehensive information on machine quilting, refer to *Machine Quilting Made Easy* by Maurine Noble (Martingale & Company, 1994).

Traditional Hand Quilting

To quilt by hand, you'll need short, sturdy needles (called *Betweens*), quilting thread, and a thimble to fit the middle finger of your sewing hand. Most quilters also use a frame or hoop to support their work. Quilting needles run from sizes 3 to 12; the higher the number, the finer and shorter the needle. Use the shortest needle you can comfortably handle; the shorter the needle, the shorter your stitches.

Thread your needle with a single strand of quilting thread about 18" long; make a small knot and insert the needle in the top layer of the quilt, about 1" from the place where you want to start stitching. Pull the needle out at the point where quilting will begin and gently pull the thread until the knot pops through the fabric and into the batting.

Begin your quilting line with a backstitch and continue with a small, even running stitch. Place your left hand underneath the quilt so you can feel the point of the needle with the tip of your finger when you take a stitch.

Push the needle through all the layers with the thimble on the middle finger of your top hand, using the dimples in the side or end of the thimble (whichever is more comfortable) to support the eye end of the needle. When you feel the tip of the needle with the middle or index finger of the underneath hand, simultaneously rock the needle eye down toward the quilt surface, depress the fabric in front of the needle with the thumb of the top hand, and push the needle tip up with the underneath finger.

When the needle tip comes through to the top of the quilt, relax the top-hand thumb and the underneath finger, rock the needle eye up so it is almost perpendicular to the quilt, and push the needle through the layers to start the next stitch. Repeat the process until you have three or four stitches on the needle, then pull the needle all the way through, taking up any slack in the thread, and start again.

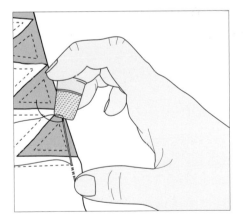

To end a line of quilting, make a small knot close to the last stitch, then backstitch, running the thread a needle's length through the batting. Gently pull the thread until the knot pops into the batting; clip the thread at the quilt's surface.

Remove basting stitches as you quilt, leaving only those that go around the outside edges of the quilt.

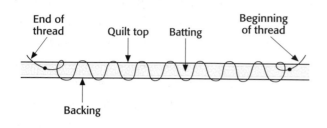

Utility Quilting

Utility quilting is faster than traditional hand quilting but homier than machine quilting; you use big needles and heavy threads—such as perle cotton, crochet thread, or several strands of embroidery floss—and take big stitches, anywhere from ⅛" to ¼" in length. This method is well worth considering for casual, scrappy quilts and for pieces you might otherwise plan to machine quilt. Quilts finished with this technique are unquestionably sturdy, and the added surface texture is very pleasing.

You can work freehand, without marking the quilt top, or you can mark quilting lines as usual. Use the shortest, finest, sharp-pointed needle you can get the thread through; try several different kinds to find the needle that works best for you. I like working with No. 8 perle cotton and a No. 6 Between needle. Keep your stitches as straight and even as possible.

Crow-Footing

I have an old comforter in my collection that is tied with a technique called *crow-footing,* or sometimes *crow's-footing.* Crow-footing is done with a long needle and thick thread, such as a single or double strand of perle cotton or crochet thread. Isolated fly stitches are worked in a grid across the surface of the quilt, leaving a small diagonal stitch on the back of the quilt; there are no visible knots or dangling threads. Stitches can be spaced as far apart as the length of your needle will allow.

Put your work in a hoop or frame. Use a long, sharp-pointed needle—try cotton darners,

milliner's needles, or soft-sculpture needles. Make a small knot in the thread and insert the needle in the top layer of the quilt about 1" from A. Pull the needle out at A and gently pull the thread until the knot pops through the fabric and into the batting. Hold the thread down with your thumb and insert the needle at B as shown; go through *all three layers* and bring the needle out at C. Insert the needle at D and travel *through the top layer only* to start the next stitch at A.

Work in rows from the top to the bottom or from the right to the left of the quilt, spacing the stitches 2" to 3" apart. To end stitching, bring the needle out at C and make a small knot about ⅛" from the surface of the quilt. Make a backstitch at D, running the thread through the batting an inch or so; pop the knot into the batting and clip the thread at the surface of the quilt.

Crow-Footing

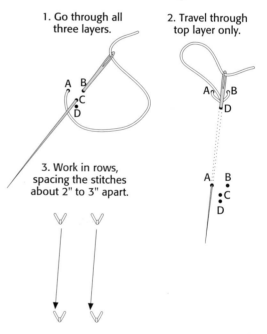

1. Go through all three layers.

2. Travel through top layer only.

3. Work in rows, spacing the stitches about 2" to 3" apart.

Backstitch Tacking

Backstitch tacking is another option. Two favorite stitches are the Mennonite tack and the Methodist knot. Both stitches are best worked from the right to the left rather than from the top to the bottom of the quilt; they leave a small horizontal stitch on the back of the quilt.

To do the Mennonite tack, bring the needle out at A and take a backstitch ¼" to ⅜" long *through all three layers,* coming back up just a few threads from the starting point (B–C). Reinsert the needle at D and travel *through the top layer only* to start the next stitch. The tiny second stitch, which should be almost invisible, crosses over the back-stitch and locks the tacking.

Mennonite Tack

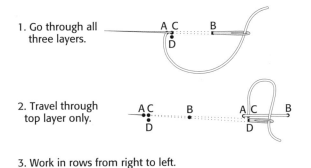

1. Go through all three layers.

2. Travel through top layer only.

3. Work in rows from right to left.

The Methodist knot is done with two back-stitches, one long and one short or both the same length. Bring the needle out at A and take a back-stitch *through all three layers,* coming back up beyond the starting point (B–C). Reinsert the needle at A and travel *through the top layer only* to start the next stitch.

Methodist Knot

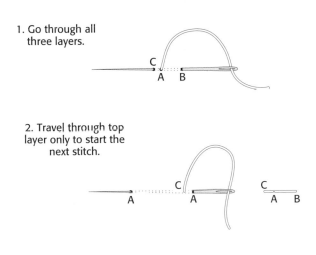

1. Go through all three layers.

2. Travel through top layer only to start the next stitch.

You can lay in any of these tacking stitches at random, rather than on a uniform grid. Early quilt-makers who used these techniques often worked with the quilt stretched full size on a large floor frame, working from both ends and rolling in the edges of the quilt as the rows of tacking were completed, thus eliminating the need for basting. You can tie or tack small quilts without basting if you spread the layers smoothly over a table or other large, flat work surface.

Other Tacking Techniques

Securing the layers of a quilt with buttons is fun and easy. Lower the feed dogs on your sewing machine and set the stitch length at 0. Adjust the stitch width to match the holes in each button. Stitch the buttons, tacking through all three layers.

Place the buttons randomly or at regular intervals, no farther apart than your batting allows. The high-loft batts commonly used for tied quilts and comforters may let you place tacks as much as 6" to 8" apart; check the manufacturer's instructions.

Use buttons in the same colors as the quilt or in contrasting colors. Shaped buttons, such as stars or hearts, add another dimension of interest.

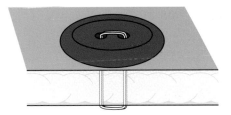

CAUTION: *Don't use buttons on quilts for babies or young children! They can create a choking hazard if pulled off.*

If your sewing machine can produce isolated decorative motifs, such as hearts or birds, you can stitch these designs through all three layers of the quilt to tack it together. As with buttons, place the motifs randomly or at regular intervals, as far apart as your batting permits. Use a single design or several; a child's quilt tacked with the letters of the alphabet would be a cozy learning tool!

Trimming and Straightening the Quilt

WHEN THE quilting or tacking is complete, remove the basting, except for the stitches around the outside edges of the quilt. Trim the batting and backing even with the edges of the quilt. Use a rotary cutter and a cutting ruler for accurate, straight edges. Make sure the corners are square.

Attaching a Hanging Sleeve

IF YOU plan to display your finished quilt on the wall, add a hanging sleeve large enough to hold a curtain rod, a dowel, or a piece of lath. Prepare the sleeve and baste it to the top of the quilt before the binding is attached, as described below.

1. Cut a piece of fabric 6" to 8" wide by the width of the quilt, piecing if necessary. Fold the short ends under ½", then ½" again; machine-hem the folded edges.

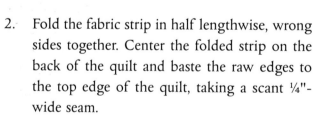

2. Fold the fabric strip in half lengthwise, wrong sides together. Center the folded strip on the back of the quilt and baste the raw edges to the top edge of the quilt, taking a scant ¼"-wide seam.

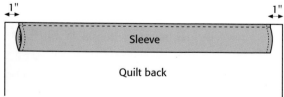

3. Bind the quilt edges as instructed in "Binding" at right, enclosing the raw edges of the sleeve. After the binding has been blindstitched in

place, push the top layer of the sleeve up so the top edge covers about half of the binding. This will provide a little give so the hanging rod doesn't put strain on the quilt itself. Blindstitch the bottom layer of the sleeve ends and the bottom edge of the sleeve in place, taking care not to catch the front of the quilt as you stitch.

4. To hang the quilt, slide a curtain rod, wooden dowel, or piece of lath through the sleeve. The larger and heavier the quilt, the thicker and sturdier the hanging rod must be. Cut the dowel or lath the width of the quilt top minus 1". Hang the quilt by resting the rod or dowel on two flat-head nails. If you're using lath, attach screw eyes or drill holes at each end, and slip the holes or eyes over small, flathead nails.

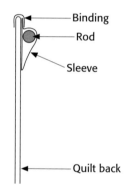

Binding

IF YOU PLAN to hang your quilt, attach a hanging sleeve to the back before attaching the binding (see "Attaching a Hanging Sleeve" at left).

In this book, fabric requirements for bindings assume ⅜"-wide (finished), double-fold binding, made from straight-grain strips cut 2½" wide and

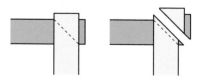

Joining Straight-Cut Strips

stitched to the outside edges of the quilt with a ⅜"-wide seam. You'll need enough binding to go around the perimeter of the quilt plus about 18". Remove the selvages from the binding strips and join the ends to make one long, continuous strip; press the seams open. Then press the strip in half lengthwise, wrong sides together.

To attach the binding to the quilt top, follow these steps:

1. Place the binding on the front of the quilt about 15" from a corner, lining up the raw edges of the binding with the raw edges of the quilt. Using a walking foot, sew the binding to the quilt with a ⅜"-wide seam; leave the first 6" of binding loose so you can more easily join the beginning and the end of the binding strip later. Be careful not to stretch the quilt or the binding as you sew. End the line of stitching ⅜" from the corner of the quilt; backstitch. Remove the quilt from the machine and clip the threads.

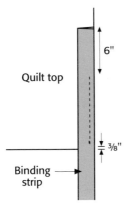

2. Turn the quilt to prepare for sewing along the next edge. Fold the binding strip at a 45° angle away from the quilt, and then fold it back on itself, keeping the raw edge even with the next edge of the quilt. There will be an angled fold at the corner; the second, straight fold should be even with the top edge of the quilt. Beginning ⅜" from the edge of the straight fold, stitch to ⅜" from the next corner,

keeping the binding aligned with the raw edge of the quilt. Fold the binding as you did at the previous corner and continue around the edge of the quilt, repeating the same procedure at the remaining corners.

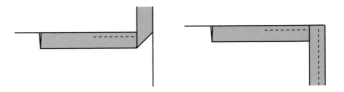

3. Approximately 10" from the starting point, stop and backstitch. Leave a 6" tail.

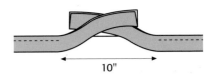

4. Fold the unstitched binding edges back on themselves so they just meet in the middle over the unsewn area of the quilt edge. Press the folds.

5. Unfold both ends of the binding. Lay the ending strip flat, right side up. Lay the beginning strip over it, right side down, matching the centers of the pressed Xs. Carefully draw a diagonal line through the point where the fold lines meet. Pin, and then stitch on the marked line.

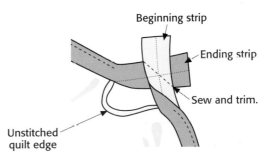

6. Check to make sure the newly seamed binding fits the unbound edge. Trim off the tail ends ¼" from the seam; press the seam open. Refold the binding, press the fold, and stitch the remainder of the binding to the quilt edge.

7. Fold the binding to the back over the raw edges of the quilt. The folded edge of the binding should just cover the stitching line. Blindstitch the binding in place, making sure your stitches don't go through to the front of the quilt. Blindstitch the folds in the miters that form at each corner, if you wish.

Quilt back

Making a Label

BE SURE to sign and date your work! At the very least, embroider your name and the year you completed the quilt on the front or back of the quilt, or incorporate this information in the quilting. One quilter I know uses her sewing machine's alphabet and number functions to stitch her name and the date on short lengths of grosgrain ribbon. She places these little labels at an angle in the bottom back corners of the quilt and secures the ends when she whips down the binding.

Future generations will want to know more than just the "who" and "when." With today's tools, it's easy to make an attractive and informative label to blindstitch to the back of your quilt. Include the name of the quilt, the maker's name, the quilter's name (if different from the maker), the city and state in which the quilt was made, the date, whom the quilt was made for and why, and any other interesting or important information about the quilt. For an antique quilt, record everything you know about the quilt, including where you purchased it.

Write the information on a piece of fabric with a reliable permanent marker, like a Pigma Micron pen. Use colored markers and add little drawings for a fancier result. Press a piece of plastic-coated freezer paper to the wrong side of your label fabric to stabilize it while you write or draw. You can draw lines on the plain side of the freezer paper with a wide-tipped marker to help you keep your writing straight.

If you have the equipment and the expertise, you can print fabric labels on a laser printer or with a photocopier. Computer printers and photocopiers that can handle index-weight paper usually can process a sheet of stabilized fabric. Iron a 9" x 12" piece of freezer paper to the back of a 9" x 12" piece of fabric, then trim this paper-and-fabric sandwich to 8½" x 11". Design your label, then print it on the fabric. Let the label stand for a few hours after it emerges from the printer or copier, and then heat-set it by pressing with a hot, dry iron. Use a pressing cloth and let the iron remain on each section of the label for at least 30 seconds.

Always test to be absolutely sure the ink used for your label is permanent. Be aware that labels that safely pass the washing-machine test sometimes bleed when they're dry-cleaned. Both handwritten and printed labels may fade with time or after repeated washings.

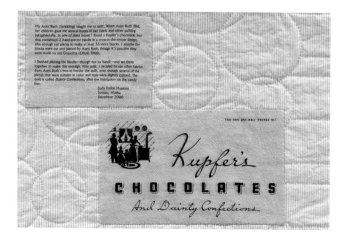

ABOUT THE QUILT PATTERNS

READ THE COMPLETE cutting and piecing instructions for the quilt you're going to make before you begin. You may want to make a sample block to test the pattern and confirm your fabric choices before you proceed.

The small arrows in the construction diagrams indicate the direction in which to press seams. When there are no arrows, press the seams however you wish.

The finished quilt dimensions in the pattern instructions may differ from the dimensions given for the pictured quilts. The pattern dimensions are based on unquilted tops that are assumed to be cut and sewn with absolute precision. The dimensions of the finished quilts in the photographs reflect reality—the compounded effects of slight inaccuracies in cutting or piecing and any stretching or take-up that might have occurred during the quilting process. Special notations describe any other significant differences between the patterns and the pictured quilts.

UNITED WE STAND

By Judy Dafoe Hopkins, 42¼" x 58¼". Quilted by Julie Fugate. My hometown has a great Fourth of July celebration, and my house is right in the thick of things. This quilt hangs outside during the festivities.

Finished Quilt Size: 42¼" x 58¼"

Materials

Yardage is based on 42"-wide fabric.

♦ 1½ yds. of medium- to large-scale blue print for top horizontal band and binding

♦ 1½ yds. of pink-and-cream star print for wide vertical strips and binding

♦ 1½ yds. of pink-blue-and-cream stripe for wide vertical strips

♦ ⅜ yd. of small-scale blue print for narrow vertical strips

♦ 1 fat quarter of pinkish cream print for appliquéd stars

♦ 3 yds. of fabric for backing (crosswise seam)

♦ 48" x 64" piece of batting

♦ Template plastic or cardboard

♦ Freezer paper

Cutting

All cutting measurements include ¼"-wide seam allowances.

From the small-scale blue print, cut:
♦ 8 selvage-to-selvage strips, 1⅛" wide

From the stripe, cut:
♦ 3 lengthwise strips, 6" x 47½"

From the star print, cut:
♦ 4 lengthwise strips, 6" x 47½"
♦ 3 lengthwise strips, 2½" x length of fabric

From the medium- to large-scale blue print, cut:
♦ 1 lengthwise strip, 11¾" x at least 44"
♦ 2 lengthwise strips, 2½" x length of fabric

Assembling the Quilt Top

1. Sew the 1⅛"-wide blue strips together end to end; press the seams open. From this pieced strip, cut 6 segments, each at least 48" long.

2. Join a 1⅛"-wide blue strip to both long edges of each stripe strip, keeping the top edges even. Trim the excess blue strips at the bottom once the seams are sewn. Press the seams toward the blue strips.

3. Join the pieced strips from step 2 with the 6"-wide star-print strips to complete the bottom section of the quilt, as shown. Press the seams toward the blue strips.

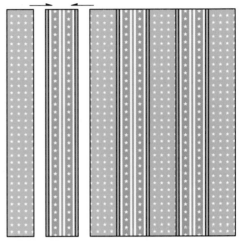

Bottom Section of Quilt

4. Measure the width of the section made in step 3 through the center. Cut the 11¾" medium- to large-scale blue print strip to the exact width measured and join it to the top edge of the bottom section of the quilt. Press the seam toward the blue print strip.

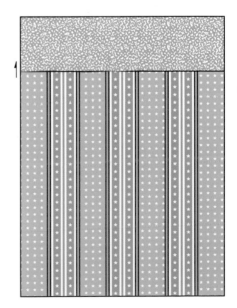

Appliquéing the Stars

See "Appliqué" on pages 14–15.

1. Trace the star appliqué pattern below onto template plastic or cardboard; cut out carefully. Mark the top and the center line (which is also the grain line) on the template. Use the template to make 13 freezer-paper stars.

2. Pin the freezer-paper stars, plastic-coated side up, to the wrong side of the pinkish cream fat quarter, leaving at least ¾" between each star. Cut out the stars, adding a ¼"-wide seam allowance around the outside edges of the freezer paper as you cut. Press the seam allowances over the edges of the paper stars, clipping the inside corners.

3. Iron the stars in place and appliqué them to the horizontal blue band as shown. Center each star in the bottom row above a wide vertical strip, positioning it so the top of the star is 4¼" above the seam that joins the horizontal band to the bottom section of the quilt. Center each star in the top row above a narrow blue vertical strip, placing it so the top of the star is 7¾" above the seam.

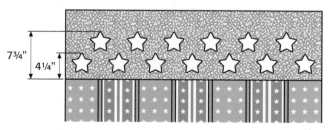

7¾"   4¼"

Appliqué 13 stars to horizontal blue band.

Layering and Finishing the Quilt

1. Divide the backing fabric into 2 equal panels. Remove the selvages and join the panels with a ½" seam to make a single, large backing piece. Press the seam open.

2. Center the batting and quilt top on the backing; baste (see "Layering and Basting the Quilt" on pages 21–22).

3. Quilt or tack as desired (see "Quilting" on pages 22–25).

4. Refer to "Binding" on pages 26–28 to prepare the 2½"-wide blue print and star-print strips for binding. Bind the top section of the quilt with the blue print strips, and the bottom section of the quilt with the star-print strips, joining the blue print and star-print strips at the seam that connects the horizontal band to the bottom section of the quilt as shown in the quilt photo.

5. Make a label and stitch it to your quilt (see "Making a Label" on page 28).

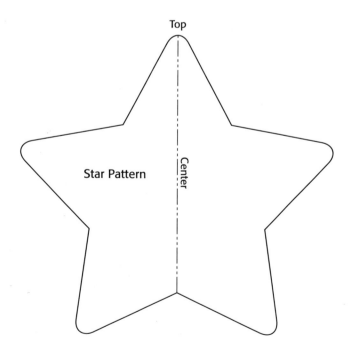

Top

Star Pattern   Center

FOREST DREAMS

By Michele A. Hall, 59½" x 72¼". Quilted by Janet Fogg. Positive-negative (counterchange) designs—where the light and dark values reverse from block to block—are always a good choice for scrappy-looking multifabric quilts.

Finished Quilt Size: 60" x 72"

Materials

Yardage is based on 42"-wide fabric.

- ✦ 1 fat quarter *each* of 8 assorted cream prints for blocks
- ✦ 1 fat quarter *each* of 8 assorted dark and/or medium green prints for blocks
- ✦ 1 yd. of green print for inner border and binding⋆
- ✦ 1½ yds. of cream print for outer border⋆
- ✦ 4¼ yds. of fabric for backing (crosswise seam)
- ✦ 66" x 78" piece of batting

⋆ *Use the same fabric as one of the fat quarters or select a different print.*

Cutting

All cutting measurements include ¼"-wide seam allowances.

From *each* of the 8 assorted cream prints and the 8 assorted green prints, cut:
- ✦ 4 strips, 2" x 21"⋆ (32 cream and 32 green strips total)
- ✦ 2 strips, 3½" x 21"⋆; crosscut each strip into 5 squares, 3½" x 3½" (80 cream and 80 green squares total)

From the green print for inner border and binding, cut:
- ✦ 7 selvage-to-selvage strips, 1½" wide
- ✦ 8 selvage-to-selvage strips, 2½" wide

From the cream print for outer border, cut:
- ✦ 8 selvage-to-selvage strips, 5½" wide

⋆ *Because the size of fat quarters can vary, the strip length (21") is approximate. Cut the strips the full length of the longest side of the fat quarter.*

Making the Blocks and Assembling the Quilt Top

1. Join each 2" x 21" cream strip to a 2" x 21" green strip to make 32 strip units as shown. Use as many different cream/green fabric combinations as possible. Press the seams toward the green fabrics. The strip units should measure 3½" wide (raw edge to raw edge) when sewn. Cut 10 segments, each 2" wide, from each strip unit (320 total).

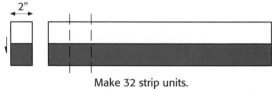

Make 32 strip units.
Cut 10 segments from each strip unit (320 total).

2. Randomly join the segments you cut in step 2 to make 160 four-patch units as shown. Press the seams however you wish. Each unit should measure 3½" x 3½" (raw edge to raw edge) when sewn.

Make 160.

3. Join a 3½" green square to 80 of the four-patch units as shown on page 35. Combine the fabrics at random. Be sure the green squares in each four-patch unit are oriented at the top left and bottom right as shown.

   Join a 3½" cream square to the remaining 80 four-patch units as shown, being sure the green squares in each four-patch unit are oriented at the top left and bottom right. Press the seams toward the 3½" green and cream squares. The units should measure 3½" x 6½" (raw edge to raw edge) when sewn.

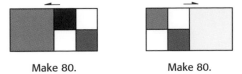

Make 80.   Make 80.

4. Randomly join the green units from step 3 to make 40 block A as shown. Randomly join the cream units from step 3 to make 40 block B as shown. Press the seams however you wish. The blocks should measure 6½" x 6½" (raw edge to raw edge) when sewn.

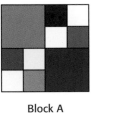

Block A   Block B
Make 40.   Make 40.

5. Join the blocks to make 10 horizontal rows, each containing 4 block A and 4 block B. Alternate the block positions from row to row as shown. Press the seams in opposite

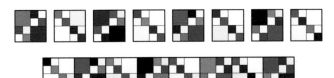

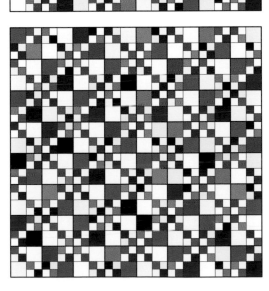

directions from row to row. Note that the blocks should be arranged so that the cream squares are running on the diagonal from lower left to upper right, and the green squares are running on the diagonal from upper left to lower right. Join the rows. Press the seams in one direction.

6. Join the inner and outer borders to the quilt (see "Borders with Straight-Cut Corners" on pages 18–19). For the inner border, seam the 1½"-wide green strips as necessary to make strips long enough to border the quilt; press the seams open. Measure the length of the quilt through the center. Cut 2 border strips to the length measured and join them to the sides of the quilt, matching the ends and centers and easing as necessary. Press the seams toward the borders. Measure the width of the quilt through the center, including the border pieces you just added. Cut 2 border strips to the width measured and join them to the top and bottom of the quilt. Press the seams toward the borders. Repeat with the 5½"-wide cream strips for the outer border.

Layering and Finishing the Quilt

1. Divide the backing fabric into 2 equal panels. Remove the selvages and join the panels with a ½" seam to make a single, large backing piece. Press the seam open.

2. Center the batting and quilt top on the backing; baste (see "Layering and Basting the Quilt" on pages 21–22).

3. Quilt or tack as desired (see "Quilting" on pages 22–25).

4. Bind the quilt with the 2½"-wide green print strips (see "Binding" on pages 26–28).

5. Make a label and stitch it to your quilt (see "Making a Label" on page 28).

TRIP AROUND THE RAIL

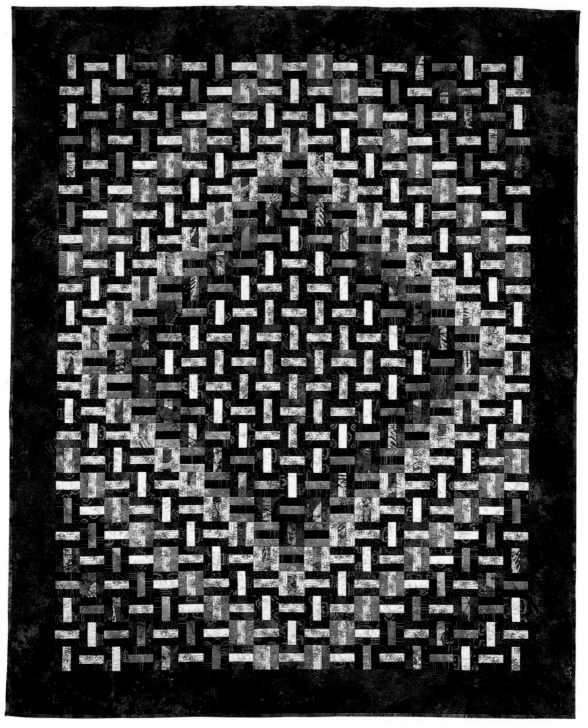

*By George Taylor, 68¼" x 86¼". Simple Rail Fence blocks and luscious berry-
and citrus-colored prints combine to make a singularly striking quilt.*

Finished Quilt Size: 68" x 86"

Materials

Yardage is based on 42"-wide fabric. Paste snips of fabrics 1–8 to an index card and number the snips for reference during the cutting-and-assembling process.

- Fabric 1: 1¾ yds. of dark red-violet print for blocks and binding
- Fabric 2: 1 yd. of a different dark red-violet print for blocks
- Fabric 3: ⅞ yd. of dark blue-violet print for blocks
- Fabric 4: 2½ yds. of a different dark blue-violet print for blocks and border
- Fabric 5: ½ yd. of medium blue-violet print for blocks
- Fabric 6: ⅝ yd. of light violet print for blocks
- Fabric 7: 1⅜ yds. of medium yellow-orange print for blocks
- Fabric 8: 1⅛ yds. of dark yellow-orange print for blocks
- 5¾ yds. of fabric for backing (lengthwise seam)
- 74" x 92" piece of batting

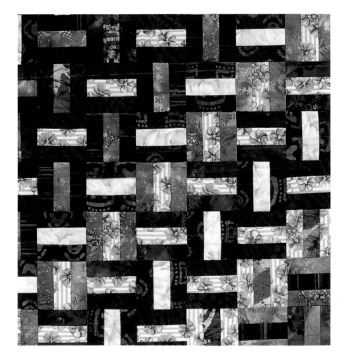

Cutting

All cutting measurements include ¼"-wide seam allowances.

From fabric 1, cut:
- 20 selvage-to-selvage strips, 1½" wide
- 9 selvage-to-selvage strips, 2½" wide

From fabric 2, cut:
- 20 selvage-to-selvage strips, 1½" wide

From fabric 3, cut:
- 17 selvage-to-selvage strips, 1½" wide

From fabric 4, cut:
- 20 selvage-to-selvage strips, 1½" wide
- 8 selvage-to-selvage strips, 6" wide

From fabric 5, cut:
- 9 selvage-to-selvage strips, 1½" wide

From fabric 6, cut:
- 10 selvage-to-selvage strips, 1½" wide

From fabric 7, cut:
- 27 selvage-to-selvage strips, 1½" wide

From fabric 8, cut:
- 21 selvage-to-selvage strips, 1½" wide

Making the Blocks and Assembling the Quilt Top

1. Join the 1½"-wide strips of fabrics 1–8 to make strip units in 8 different fabric combinations as specified in the illustrations on page 38. When you have finished joining all the strips, you will have a total of 48 strip units. Press the seams however you wish. The strip units should measure 3½" wide (raw edge to raw edge) when sewn

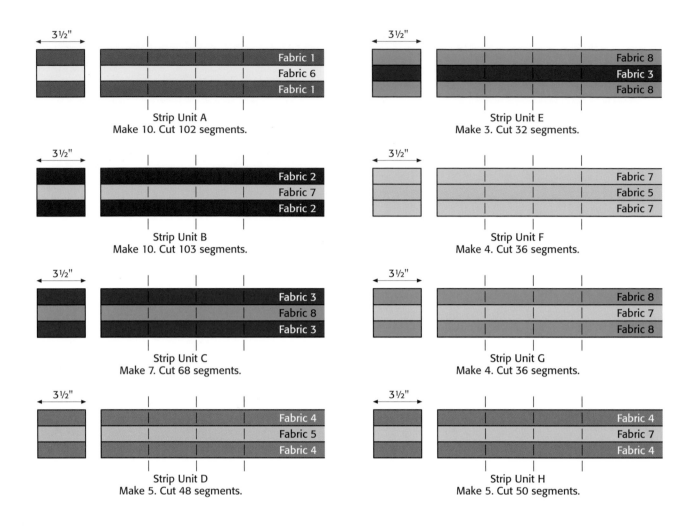

Strip Unit A
Make 10. Cut 102 segments.

Strip Unit E
Make 3. Cut 32 segments.

Strip Unit B
Make 10. Cut 103 segments.

Strip Unit F
Make 4. Cut 36 segments.

Strip Unit C
Make 7. Cut 68 segments.

Strip Unit G
Make 4. Cut 36 segments.

Strip Unit D
Make 5. Cut 48 segments.

Strip Unit H
Make 5. Cut 50 segments.

Cut each strip unit into the number of 3½"-wide segments indicated. When you have finished cutting all the 3½" segments, you will have a total of 475 Rail Fence blocks, each measuring 3½" x 3½" (raw edge to raw edge). Place matching blocks together and label them with their strip-unit letter to facilitate quilt assembly.

2. On a floor or design wall, arrange the Rail Fence blocks according to the quilt plan on the facing page. The letters in the squares match the strip-unit letters.

The quilt plan represents the top half of the quilt plus the center row. Once you have laid out the first 12 rows and the center row, continue laying out the rows in reverse order (i.e., repeat row 12 after the center row, and then row 11 and so forth, until you reach the last row, which is a repeat of row 1). Once the rows are laid out, check to see that the pattern looks right and that all the blocks are oriented correctly.

3. Join the blocks into rows. Press the seams in opposite directions from row to row. Join the rows. Press the seams in one direction.

4. Join the border to the quilt (see "Borders with Straight-Cut Corners" on pages 18–19): Seam the 6"-wide fabric-4 strips as necessary to make strips long enough to border the quilt; press the seams open. Measure the length of

Row 1
Row 2
Row 3
Row 4
Row 5
Row 6
Row 7
Row 8
Row 9
Row 10
Row 11
Row 12
Center Row

Top Half of Quilt

the quilt through the center. Cut 2 border strips to the length measured and join them to the sides of the quilt, matching the ends and centers and easing as necessary. Press the seams toward the borders. Measure the width of the quilt through the center, including the border pieces you just added. Cut 2 border strips to the width measured and join them to the top and bottom of the quilt; press the seams toward the borders.

Layering and Finishing the Quilt

1. Divide the backing fabric into 2 equal panels. Remove the selvages and join the panels with a ½" seam to make a single, large backing piece. Press the seam open.

2. Center the batting and quilt top on the backing; baste (see "Layering and Basting the Quilt" on pages 21–22).

3. Quilt or tack as desired (see "Quilting" on pages 22–25).

4. Bind the quilt with the 2½"-wide fabric-1 strips (see "Binding" on pages 26–28).

5. Make a label and stitch it to your quilt (see "Making a Label" on page 28).

Patch Patch Patch

By Judy Dafoe Hopkins, 51¾" x 74¾". Quilted by Julie Kimberlin. While the red and green 25-Patch blocks are the focus of this quilt, the large sashing and border pieces give the soft multicolor background print a chance to shine.

Finished Quilt Size: 52½" x 76½"

Materials

Yardage is based on 42"-wide fabric.

- 3½ yds. of yellow tulip print for blocks, sashing pieces, and border
- ½ yd. *each* of 4 assorted green prints for blocks and binding
- ¼ yd. *each* of 4 assorted red prints for blocks
- 5 yds. of fabric for backing (lengthwise seam)
- 58" x 82" piece of batting

Cutting

All cutting measurements include ¼"-wide seam allowances.

From the yellow tulip print, cut:
- 21 selvage-to-selvage strips, 2" wide; cut each strip in half widthwise (42 strips total)
- 7 selvage-to-selvage strips, 5" wide
- Reserve the remaining fabric for sashing.

From each of the red prints, cut:
- 3 selvage-to-selvage strips, 2" wide (12 total); cut each strip in half widthwise (24 strips total)

From each of the green prints, cut:
- 3 selvage-to-selvage strips, 2" wide (12 total); cut each strip in half widthwise (24 strips total). You will use 22 strips and have 2 left over.
- 2 selvage-to-selvage strips, 2½" wide (8 total)

Making the Blocks

1. Join 2"-wide red strips and 2"-wide yellow strips to make 4 strip unit A and 3 strip unit B as shown. Use a variety of red strips in each strip unit. Press the seams toward the red strips. The strip units should measure 8" wide (raw edge to raw edge) when sewn. From each strip unit, cut the number of 2"-wide segments indicated below.

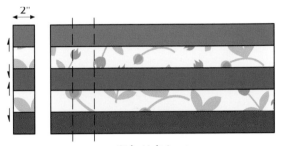

Strip Unit A
Make 4. Cut 36 segments.

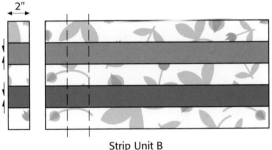

Strip Unit B
Make 3. Cut 24 segments.

2. Join the segments you cut in step 1 to make 12 block A as shown. Press the seams however you wish. The blocks should measure 8" x 8" (raw edge to raw edge) when sewn.

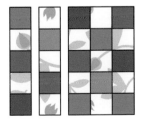
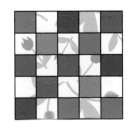

Block A
Make 12.

3. Join 2"-wide green and yellow strips to make 4 strip unit C and 3 strip unit D as shown. Use a variety of green strips in each strip unit. Press the seams toward the green strips. The strip units should measure 8" wide (raw edge to raw edge) when sewn. Cut the number of 2"-wide segments indicated below from each strip unit.

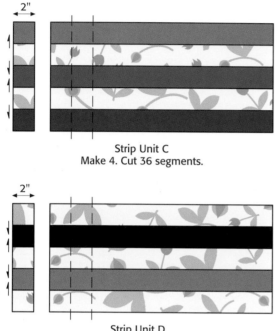

Strip Unit C
Make 4. Cut 36 segments.

Strip Unit D
Make 3. Cut 24 segments.

4. Join the segments you cut in step 3 to make 12 block B as shown. Press the seams however you wish. The blocks should measure 8" x 8" (raw edge to raw edge) when sewn.

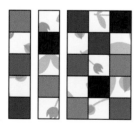

Block B
Make 12.

5. Join the remaining 2"-wide red, green, and yellow strips to make 4 strip unit E and 2 strip unit F as shown. Press the seams away from the yellow strips. The strip units should measure 5" wide (raw edge to raw edge) when sewn. Cut the number of 2"-wide segments indicated from each strip unit.

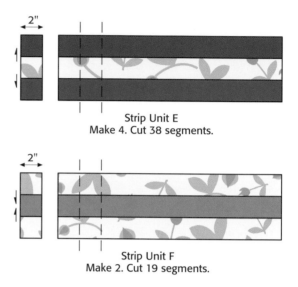

Strip Unit E
Make 4. Cut 38 segments.

Strip Unit F
Make 2. Cut 19 segments.

6. Join the segments you cut in step 5 to make 19 block C as shown. The blocks should measure 5" x 5" (raw edge to raw edge) when sewn.

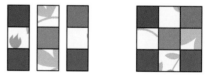

Block C
Make 19.

Assembling the Quilt Top

1. Measure blocks A, B, and C through the centers to determine the width to cut the sashing strips. If your blocks were stitched perfectly, blocks A and B should measure 8" square (raw edge to raw edge) and block C should measure 5" square (raw edge to raw edge). However, they might be a little larger or smaller. If the blocks measure several different sizes, determine the average measurement of blocks A and B and the average measurement of block C.

2. From the remaining yellow tulip fabric, cut 5 selvage-to-selvage strips the width determined in step 1 for blocks A and B (8" if your blocks came out perfectly; otherwise, use the average measurement.)

3. From the strips you cut in step 2, cut 38 segments exactly the same width as your block C measurement (5" if your blocks came out just right; otherwise, use the average measurement).

4. Join the blocks and sashing pieces into rows as shown. If you used average measurements, you can take care of any minor discrepancies by easing either the blocks or the sashing strips as you sew. Press all the seams toward the sashing strips. Note that block C should be arranged so that all of the red squares are running on the diagonal from upper left to lower right. You will have 4 block C left over to use for the border corner squares. Join the rows. Press the seams in one direction.

5. Join the border to the quilt (see "Borders with Corner Squares" on page 19): Seam the 5"-wide yellow strips as necessary to make strips long enough to border the quilt; press the seams open. Measure the length and width of the quilt through the center. Cut 2 border strips to the length measured and 2 border strips to the width measured. Join the lengthwise-measured strips to the sides of the quilt, matching the ends and centers and easing as necessary; press the seams toward the borders. Join 1 block C to each end of the widthwise-measured strips, arranging the blocks so that all of the red squares run on the diagonal from upper left to lower right; press the seams toward the border strips. Stitch these units to the top and bottom edges of the quilt; press the seams toward the borders.

Layering and Finishing the Quilt

1. Divide the backing fabric into 2 equal panels. Remove the selvages and join the panels with a ½" seam to make a single, large backing piece. Press the seam open.

2. Center the batting and quilt top on the backing; baste (see "Layering and Basting the Quilt" on pages 21–22).

3. Quilt or tack as desired (see "Quilting" on pages 22–25).

4. Stitch the 2½"-wide assorted green print strips together to make one continuous strip and bind the quilt (see "Binding" on pages 26–28).

5. Make a label and stitch it to your quilt (see "Making a Label" on page 28).

STRING STRIPPIE

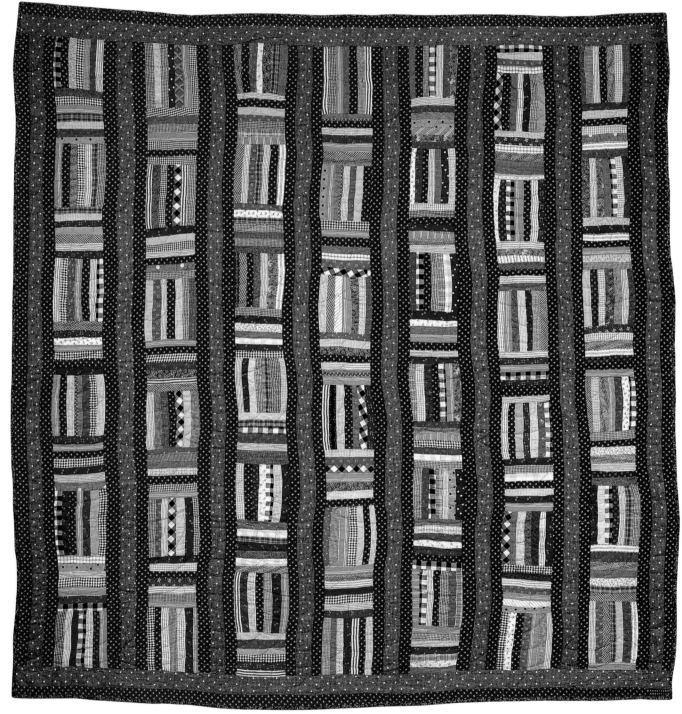

Maker unknown, circa 1920, 72½" x 77". Obviously made from clothes-making leftovers or worn-out clothes, this charming utility quilt sports an assortment of ginghams and other shirting fabrics. Collection of Jeanie Smith.

Finished Quilt Size: 70¾" x 70½"

Materials

Yardage is based on 42"-wide fabric.

- ⅛ to ½ yd. *each* of assorted gray, medium blue, tan, light blue, white, ivory, lavender, and pink prints to total 3⅜ yds. for blocks★
- 2¼ yds. of maroon print for blocks, vertical bars, and border
- 1⅜ yds. of gray print for vertical bars and border
- 4¾ yds. of fabric for backing (lengthwise or crosswise seam)
- ⅞ yd. of white-on-black print for binding
- 76" x 76" piece of batting

★*Use mostly stripes, ginghams, plaids, and checks.*

Cutting

All cutting measurements include ¼"-wide seam allowances.

From the assorted prints, cut a total of:
- 88 selvage-to-selvage strips, 1¼" wide

From the maroon print, cut:
- 10 selvage-to-selvage strips, 1¼" wide
- 32 selvage-to-selvage strips, 1¾" wide

From the gray print, cut:
- 18 selvage-to-selvage strips, 2¼" wide

From the white-on-black print, cut:
- 8 selvage-to-selvage strips, 2½" wide

Making the Blocks

1. Join the 1¼"-wide assorted and maroon strips in groups of 7 to make 14 strip units as shown. Use as many different fabric combinations as possible; include 1 maroon strip in 10 of the strip units. Press the seams in one direc-

tion. The strip units should measure 5¾" wide (raw edge to raw edge) when sewn.

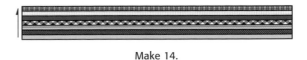

Make 14.

2. From *each* of 6 of the strip units from step 1, cut 2 segments 7¼" wide, 2 segments 6½" wide, and 2 segments 6" wide (12 segments total of each width).

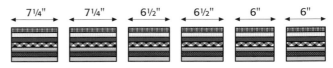

From each of 6 strip units, cut segments as shown.

3. From one of the strip units from step 1, cut 3 segments 7¼" wide and 2 segments 6½" wide. This will give you a total of fifteen 7¼" segments and fourteen 6½" segments.

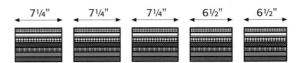

From 1 strip unit, cut segments as shown.

4. From the 7 remaining strip units, cut a total of 37 segments, each 5¾" wide. Count the pieces as you cut; don't cut to the end of the seventh strip.

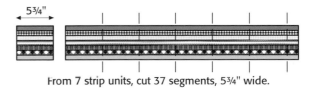

From 7 strip units, cut 37 segments, 5¾" wide.

5. From the remainder of the seventh strip from step 4, cut 1 segment, 6½" wide.

Cut 1 segment, 6½" wide.

Assembling the Quilt Top

1. Join the blocks in vertical rows to make 5 row A and 2 row B as shown.

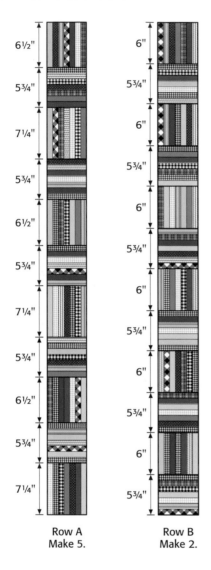

Row A
Make 5.

Row B
Make 2.

2. Join 7 of the 1¾"-wide maroon strips end to end to make a long, continuous strip. Press the seams open. Repeat to make a total of 4 maroon strips. Join 7 of the 2¼"-wide gray strips end to end to make a long, continuous strip. Repeat to make a second gray strip.

Stitch maroon strips to each side of the gray strips as shown, staggering the seams, to make 2 long strip units. Press the seams toward the gray strips.

3. Measure the length of each row A and row B strip through the vertical center. Each row will measure 65" long (raw edge to raw edge) if sewn perfectly. However, your rows may be a little longer or shorter. If the rows measure several different lengths, determine the average length.

4. From the maroon-and-gray strip units, cut 8 segments to the length determined in step 3.

5. Join the segments from step 4 and rows A and B as shown on the facing page, reversing the rows where indicated. If you used the average row measurement, you can take care of any minor discrepancies by easing either the rows or the vertical bars as you sew. Press the seams toward the step 4 vertical bars.

6. Join the 4 remaining 1¾"-wide maroon strips end to end to make one continuous strip. Press the seams open. Repeat with the 4 remaining 2¼"-wide gray strips. Join the strips as shown to make the border strip unit, staggering the seams. Press the seam toward the maroon strip.

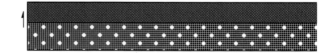

7. Measure the width of the quilt through the center. From the border strip unit you made in step 6, cut 2 segments the width measured and stitch the strips to the top and bottom of the quilt. Place the gray strip closest to the quilt. Press the seams toward the borders.

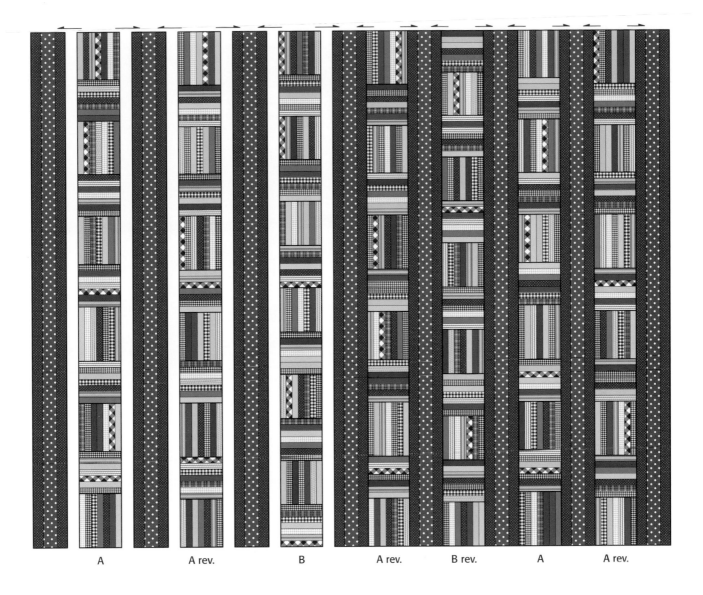

A   A rev.   B   A rev.   B rev.   A   A rev.

Layering and Finishing the Quilt

1. Divide the backing fabric into 2 equal panels. Remove the selvages and join the panels with a ½" seam to make a single, large backing piece. Press the seam open.

2. Center the batting and quilt top on the backing; baste (see "Layering and Basting the Quilt" on pages 21–22).

3. Quilt or tack as desired (see "Quilting" on pages 22–25).

4. Bind the quilt with the 2½"-wide white-on-black print strips (see "Binding" on pages 26–28).

5. Make a label and stitch it to your quilt (see "Making a Label" on page 28).

DAINTY CONFECTIONS

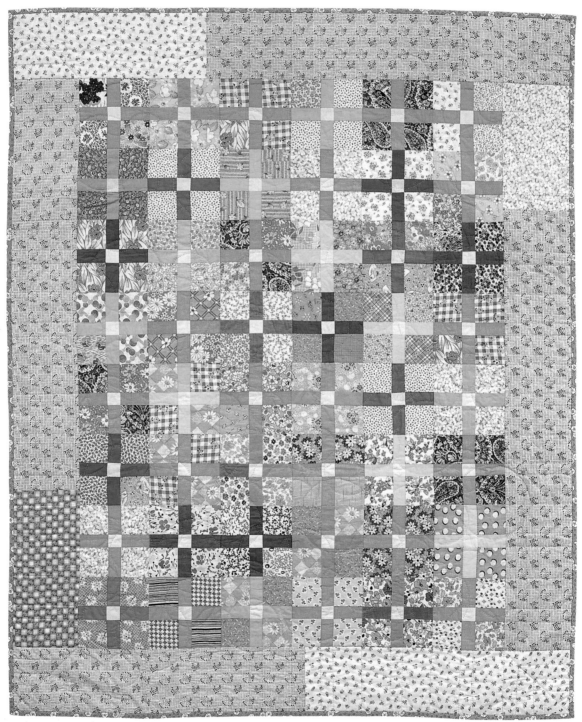

By Olive Smith, Ruth Strickling, and Judy Dafoe Hopkins, 47¾" x 59¾". Quilted by Julie Kimberlin.

The blocks and partial blocks found in a candy box labeled "Dainty Confections" probably were made by my grandmother,

Olive Smith, or my aunt, Ruth Strickling. I finished the blocks and put the quilt together.

Finished Quilt Size: 48" x 60"

Materials

Yardage is based on 42"-wide fabric.

♦ ¼ to ½ yd. *each* of 4 assorted prints to total 1½ yds. for border*

♦ ¼ yd. of muslin for blocks

♦ 1 strip, exactly 3" wide and at least 39" long, *each* of 4 assorted green solids for blocks

♦ 1 strip, exactly 3" wide and at least 33" long, *each* of 1 yellow and 1 orange solid for blocks

♦ 1 strip, exactly 3" wide and at least 27" long, *each* of 1 light pink and 1 lavender solid for blocks

♦ 1 strip, exactly 3" wide and at least 15" long, *each* of 1 hot pink, 1 blue, and 1 red solid for blocks

♦ 1 strip, exactly 3" wide and at least 14" long, *each* of 48 assorted prints for blocks**

♦ 3½ yds. of fabric for backing (crosswise seam)

♦ ⅝ yd. mint green print for binding

♦ 54" x 66" piece of batting

Use some of the same fabrics you used for the blocks or completely different fabrics.
**Use the same fabric more than once if you wish.*

Cutting

All cutting measurements include ¼"-wide seam allowances.

From the muslin, cut:

♦ 2 selvage-to-selvage strips, 1½" wide; cross-cut the strips to make 48 squares, 1½" x 1½"

From *each* of the 3"-wide assorted green solid strips, cut:

♦ 24 rectangles, 1½" x 3" (96 total)

From *each* of the 3"-wide yellow and orange solid strips, cut:

♦ 20 rectangles, 1½" x 3" (20 yellow and 20 orange total)

From *each* of the 3"-wide light pink and lavender solid strips, cut:

♦ 16 rectangles, 1½" x 3" (16 light pink and 16 lavender total)

From *each* of the 3"-wide hot pink, blue, and red solid strips, cut:

♦ 8 rectangles, 1½" x 3" (8 hot pink, 8 blue, and 8 red total)

From *each* of the 3"-wide assorted print strips, cut:

♦ 4 squares, 3" x 3" (192 total)

From the assorted prints for border, cut a *total* of:

♦ 6 selvage-to-selvage strips, 6½" wide

From the mint green print, cut:

♦ 6 selvage-to-selvage strips, 2½" wide

Making the Blocks and Assembling the Quilt Top

BECAUSE THERE are so many different fabric combinations in the blocks, strip-piecing methods are not efficient for this quilt. Note that in the pictured quilt, just one fabric is used for the large squares in some of the blocks. In other blocks, two different fabrics, often arranged asymmetrically, are used for the large print squares.

1. Join 4 solid rectangles (all the same color), 4 print squares (all the same print or two different prints), and 1 muslin square as shown on page 50. Press the seams in the directions indicated. Repeat with another group of fabrics until you have completed 48 blocks. The

blocks should measure 6½" x 6½" (raw edge to raw edge) when sewn.

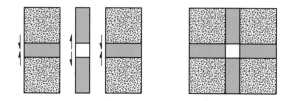

2. Join the blocks to make 8 horizontal rows of 6 blocks each, arranging the blocks so that every other one has a green cross in the center as shown. Press the seams in opposite directions from row to row. Join the rows. Press the seams in one direction.

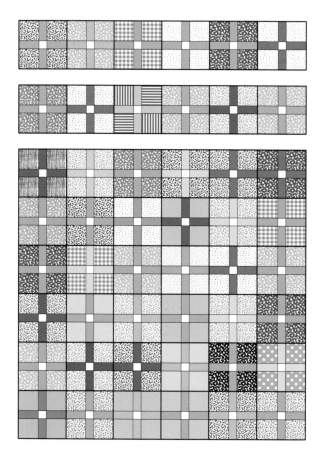

3. Cut the 6½"-wide border strips into random lengths and join them end to end to make 4 border strips, each at least 50" long. Press the seams open.

4. Join the border strips to the quilt (see "Borders with Straight-Cut Corners" on pages 18–19): Measure the length of the quilt through the center. Cut 2 pieced border strips to the length measured and join them to the sides of the quilt, matching the ends and centers and easing as necessary; press the seams toward the borders. Measure the width of the quilt through the center, including the border pieces you just added. Cut 2 border strips to the width measured and join them to the top and bottom of the quilt; press the seams toward the borders.

Layering and Finishing the Quilt

1. Divide the backing fabric into 2 equal panels. Remove the selvages and join the panels with a ½" seam to make a single, large backing piece. Press the seam open.

2. Center the batting and quilt top on the backing; baste (see "Layering and Basting the Quilt" on pages 21–22).

3. Quilt or tack as desired (see "Quilting" on pages 22–25).

4. Bind the quilt with the 2½"-wide mint green print strips (see "Binding" on pages 26–28).

5. Make a label and stitch it to your quilt (see "Making a Label" on page 28).

DANDELION WINE

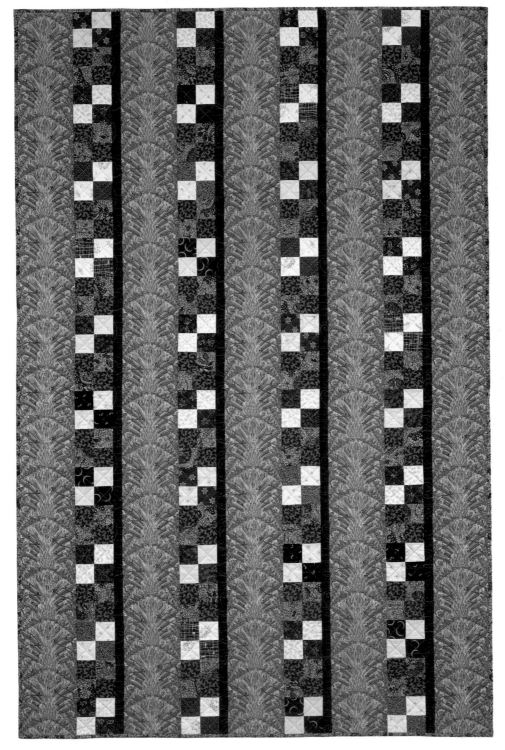

By Judy Dafoe Hopkins, 55¼" x 84". Quilted by Becky Crook. A close look at the wide vertical bars reveals an unusual dandelion print that languished in my I-wonder-what-to-do-with-this-fabric pile for several years (detail on page 29).

Finished Quilt Size: 57" x 85½"

Materials

Yardage is based on 42"-wide fabric.

♦ 2⅞ yds. of dandelion print (or other interesting print) for wide vertical bars

♦ 1¼ yds. of tan print for blocks and binding

♦ 1 strip, exactly 2¾" wide x at least 24" long, *each* of 10 assorted light prints for blocks*

♦ 1 strip, exactly 2¾" wide x at least 24" long, *each* of 10 assorted dark prints (greens, blues, reds) for blocks

♦ ½ yd. of dark brown print for narrow vertical bars

♦ ⅝ yd. of dark tan print for blocks

♦ 5¾ yds. of fabric for backing (lengthwise seam)

♦ 63" x 91" piece of batting

*Use the same print more than once if you wish.

Cutting

All cutting measurements include ¼"-wide seam allowances.

From the tan print, cut:
♦ 6 selvage-to-selvage strips, 2¾" wide
♦ 8 selvage-to-selvage strips, 2½" wide

From the dark tan print, cut:
♦ 6 selvage-to-selvage strips, 2¾" wide

From the dark brown print, cut:
♦ 9 selvage-to-selvage strips, 1½" wide

From the dandelion print, cut:
♦ 5 lengthwise strips, 7½" x at least 88"

Making the Blocks

1. Randomly join the 2¾"-wide assorted light strips to the 2¾"-wide assorted dark strips to make 10 light-and-dark strip units as shown. Press the seams toward the dark strips. The strip units should measure 5" wide (raw edge to raw edge) when sewn. Cut 8 segments, 2¾" wide, from each strip unit (80 total).

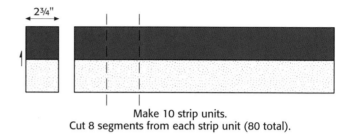

2¾"

Make 10 strip units.
Cut 8 segments from each strip unit (80 total).

2. Join 2 identical segments from step 1 to make 1 unit A as shown. Repeat with the remaining segments from step 1 for a total of 40 unit A. The units should measure 5" x 5" (raw edge to raw edge) when sewn.

Unit A
Make 40 total.

3. Join the 2¾"-wide tan print strips to the 2¾"-wide dark tan print strips to make 6 strip units as shown. Press the seams toward the dark tan strips. The strip units should measure 5" wide (raw edge to raw edge) when sewn. From these strip units, cut 72 segments, 2¾" wide.

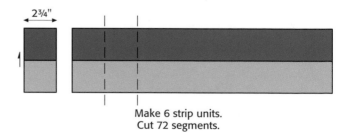

2¾"

Make 6 strip units.
Cut 72 segments.

4. Join the segments from step 3 to make 36 unit B as shown. Press the seams however you wish. The units should measure 5" x 5" (raw edge to raw edge) when sewn.

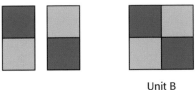

Unit B
Make 36.

Assembling the Quilt Top

1. Join units A and B to make 4 vertical rows, each row containing 10 unit A and 9 unit B as shown at right. Press the seams however you wish.

2. Sew the 1½"-wide dark brown print strips together end to end to make one continuous strip. Press the seams open. From the continuous strip, cut 4 equal pieces, each about 89" long. Join these strips to the left sides of 4 of the dandelion-print strips, matching the top edges. Trim the excess dark brown strip at the bottom edges. Press the seams toward the dandelion strips.

3. Measure the length of the unit A-B rows through the vertical center. Each row will measure 86" long (raw edge to raw edge) if sewn perfectly. However, your rows may be a little longer or shorter. If your unit A-B rows measure several different lengths, determine the average length.

4. Cut the 4 pieced bars you made in step 2 and the remaining 7½"-wide dandelion print strip to the length determined in step 3.

5. Join the pieced bars and the strip you cut in step 4 to the unit A-B rows as shown. If you used the average row measurement, you can take care of any minor discrepancies by easing either the rows or the bars as you sew. Press the seams away from the A-B rows.

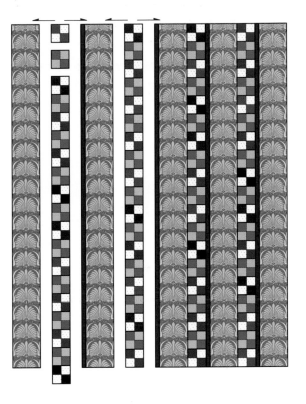

Layering and Finishing the Quilt

1. Divide the backing fabric into 2 equal panels. Remove the selvages and join the panels with a ½" seam to make a single, large backing piece. Press the seam open.

2. Center the batting and quilt top on the backing; baste (see "Layering and Basting the Quilt" on pages 21–22).

3. Quilt or tack as desired (see "Quilting" on pages 22–25).

4. Bind the quilt with the 2½"-wide tan print strips (see "Binding" on pages 26–28).

5. Make a label and stitch it to your quilt (see "Making a Label" on page 28).

MAGGIE'S QUILT

By George Taylor, 42" x 56½". George used scraps in colors from the Pennsylvania Amish palette and an interesting linear print for this lively baby gift. Collection of Maggie French; photo by Sharon Risedorph.

Finished Quilt Size: 45" x 60"

Materials

Yardage is based on 42"-wide fabric.

- ✦ 2 yds. of black print for plain squares and binding
- ✦ 1 fat quarter *each* of medium pink, dark pink, light violet, medium violet, dark violet, and medium blue-green solids for blocks
- ✦ ⅞ yd. of turquoise solid for blocks
- ✦ ½ yd. of light pink solid for blocks
- ✦ 3¼ yds. fabric for backing (crosswise seam)
- ✦ 51" x 66" piece of batting

Cutting

All cutting measurements include ¼"-wide seam allowances.

From the light pink solid, cut:
- ✦ 7 selvage-to-selvage strips, 1¾" wide; cut the strips in half widthwise (14 strips total)

From the turquoise solid, cut:
- ✦ 14 selvage-to-selvage strips, 1¾" wide; cut the strips in half widthwise (28 strips total)

From *each* of the 6 fat quarters, cut:
- ✦ 7 strips, 1¾" x 21"* (42 total)

From the black print, cut:
- ✦ 11 selvage-to-selvage strips, 4¼" wide; cut the strips into 96 squares, 4¼" x 4¼"
- ✦ 6 selvage-to-selvage strips, 2½" wide

*Because the size of fat quarters can vary, the strip length (21") is approximate. Cut the strips the full length of the longest side of the fat quarter.

Making the Blocks and Assembling the Quilt Top

1. Join 1¾"-wide light pink strips and 1¾"-wide turquoise strips to make 2 strip unit A and 1 strip unit B as shown. Press the seams toward the turquoise strips. The strip units should measure 4¼" wide (raw edge to raw edge) when sewn. From each strip unit, cut the number of 1¾"-wide segments indicated below.

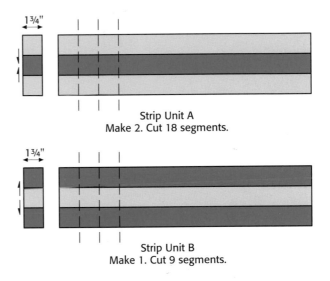

Strip Unit A
Make 2. Cut 18 segments.

Strip Unit B
Make 1. Cut 9 segments.

2. Join the segments from strip units A and B to make 9 Nine Patch blocks as shown. Press the seams however you wish. The blocks should measure 4¼" x 4¼" (raw edge to raw edge) when sewn.

Make 9.

3. Repeat steps 1 and 2 with the following combinations of 1¾"-wide strips; press seams toward the turquoise strips. Make 9 blocks of each combination (54 blocks). You will now have a total of 63 blocks with turquoise crosses in the center.

Strip Unit A (Make 2 of each.)
- Medium pink—turquoise—medium pink
- Dark pink—turquoise—dark pink
- Light violet—turquoise—light violet
- Medium violet—turquoise—medium violet
- Dark violet—turquoise—dark violet
- Medium blue-green—turquoise—medium blue-green

Strip Unit B (Make 1 of each.)
- Turquoise—medium pink—turquoise
- Turquoise—dark pink—turquoise
- Turquoise—light violet—turquoise
- Turquoise—medium violet—turquoise
- Turquoise—dark violet—turquoise
- Turquoise—medium blue-green—turquoise

Make 9.　　Make 9.　　Make 9.

Make 9.　　Make 9.　　Make 9.

4. Cut each of the remaining 1¾"-wide strips into 3 pieces, each at least 6½" long. When you have cut all the strips, you will have 27 light pink pieces and 6 pieces each of the fat-quarter colors.

5. Using the 1¾" x 6½" (or longer) pieces from step 4, refer to step 1 to make strip units A and B in the following combinations. Press the seams in each strip unit toward the darker strip.

Strip Unit A (Make 2 of each.)
- Medium pink—light pink—medium pink
- Dark pink—light pink—dark pink
- Light violet—light pink—light violet
- Medium violet—light pink—medium violet
- Dark violet—light pink—dark violet
- Medium blue-green—light pink—medium blue-green

Strip Unit B (Make 1 of each.)
- Light pink—medium pink—light pink
- Light pink—dark pink—light pink
- Light pink—light violet—light pink
- Light pink—medium violet—light pink
- Light pink—dark violet—light pink
- Light pink—medium blue-green—light pink

6. Cut six 1¾"-wide segments from each strip unit A combination and three 1¾"-wide segments from each strip unit B combination. Make 3 blocks in each color combination. You will have a total of 18 blocks with light pink crosses in the center.

Make 3.　　Make 3.　　Make 3.

Make 3.　　Make 3.　　Make 3.

7. Make 15 more Nine Patch blocks in the fabric combinations of your choice. Make mostly 2-fabric blocks, but note that the pictured quilt includes several scrappy, multifabric blocks. Start by cutting 1 or 2 more 1¾"-wide strips from the remaining piece of each of the 6 fat quarters. Cut these strips into pieces at least 4" long, and join these pieces to make assorted 3-strip strip units. Cut 1¾"-wide segments from these strip units and from any leftover strip units from steps 1, 3, and 6, and join them to make the 15 needed blocks.

8. Join the blocks and the black print squares to make 16 horizontal rows of 6 Nine Patch blocks and 6 black squares each, alternating the position of the blocks in every other row as shown. Press the seams toward the black print squares. Join the rows. Press the seams in one direction.

Layering and Finishing the Quilt

1. Divide the backing fabric into 2 equal panels. Remove the selvages and join the panels with a ½" seam to make a single, large backing piece. Press the seam open.

2. Center the batting and quilt top on the backing; baste (see "Layering and Basting the Quilt" on pages 21–22).

3. Quilt or tack as desired (see "Quilting" on pages 22–25).

4. Bind the quilt with the 2½"-wide black print strips (see "Binding" on pages 26–28).

5. Make a label and stitch it to your quilt (see "Making a Label" on page 28).

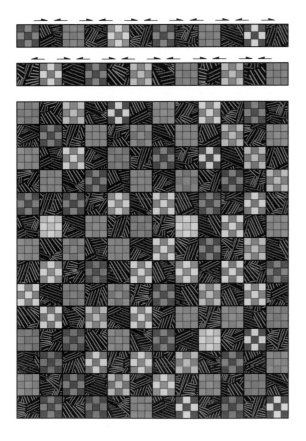

PETER'S QUILT

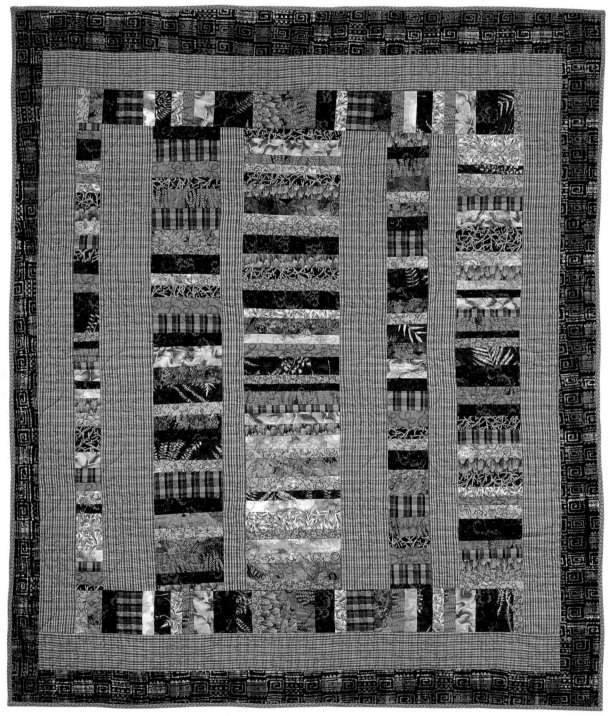

By Tina Tomsen, 62¾" x 73½". Quilted by Carol Hill. Made from strips left over from another project, this quilt is an informal interpretation of the Chinese Coins design. Collection of Peter Hale.

Finished Quilt Size: 47½" x 56"

Note that the instructions given are for a crib-size quilt, which is smaller than the one pictured at left. The quilt will look the same, but the reduced size allows for more efficient use of fabric.

Materials

Yardage is based on 42"-wide fabric.

♦ 1 fat quarter *each* of 8 assorted green, blue, and purple prints, ranging from light to dark, for pieced bars

♦ 1½ yds. of blue-and-gray plaid for vertical bars, inner border, and binding

♦ ⅞ yd. of dark blue print for outer border

♦ 3½ yds. of fabric for backing (crosswise seam)

♦ 53" x 62" piece of batting

Cutting

All cutting measurements include ¼"-wide seam allowances.

From each of the fat quarters, cut:
♦ 1 strip, 1¼" x 21"* (8 total)
♦ 1 strip, 1½" x 21"* (8 total)
♦ 2 strips, 2" x 21"* (16 total)
♦ 1 strip, 2½" x 21"* (8 total)
♦ 1 strip, 2¾" x 21"* (8 total)

From the blue-and-gray plaid, cut:
♦ 1 lengthwise strip, 4½" x about 38"
♦ 1 lengthwise strip, 4" x about 38"
♦ 1 lengthwise strip, 2¾" x about 38"
♦ 1 lengthwise strip, 2¼" x about 38"
♦ 4 lengthwise strips, 3½" x length of fabric
♦ 5 lengthwise strips, 2½" x length of fabric

From the dark blue print, cut:
♦ 6 selvage-to-selvage strips, 4" wide

Because the size of fat quarters can vary, the strip length (21") is approximate. Cut the strips the full length of the longest side of the fat quarter.

Making the Pieced Bars

1. Separate the fat-quarter strips according to width. Pick up 6 strips from your strip piles: 1 *each* of the 1¼"-, 1½"-, 2½"-, and 2¾"-wide strips and 2 of the 2"-wide strips. Join these strips along the long edges to make a strip unit as shown, combining the fabrics and strip widths at random. Make 8 strip units total, varying the fabrics and the order in which the strip widths are joined. Press the seams however you wish. Each strip unit should measure 9½" wide (raw edge to raw edge) when sewn.

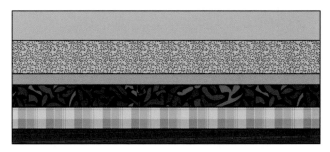

Make 8 total, varying the order in which strip widths are joined.

2. From *each* of 4 of the strip units from step 1, cut 1 segment 6" wide, 1 segment 4" wide, 1 segment 3½" wide, and 1 segment 2½" wide as shown. When you have cut all 4 strip units, you will have a total of four 6"-wide segments, four 4"-wide segments, four 3½"-wide segments, and four 2½"-wide segments.

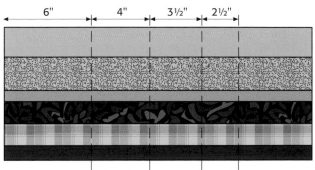

From 4 strip units, cut segments as shown.

3. From *each* of the remaining 4 strip units, cut 1 segment 8" wide, 1 segment 5½" wide, and 1 segment 4" wide as shown. When you have cut all 4 strip units, you will have a total of four 8"-wide segments, four 5½"-wide segments, and four 4"-wide segments.

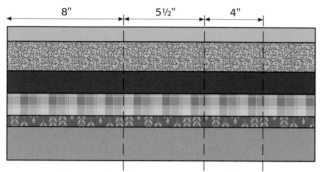

From 4 strip units, cut segments as shown.

4. Join 4 segments of each size along the short edges to make pieced bars that measure about 36½" long as shown. For instance, you have 4 segments that are 6" wide. Stitch them along the short (6") edges to make one continuous strip that will end up being 6" wide by about 36½" long. Make 2 bars from the 4"-wide segments and 1 bar *each* from the segments in the remaining widths (7 bars total).

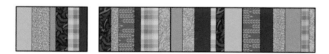

Make 7 total.

Assembling the Quilt Top

1. Set aside the two 4"-wide pieced bars. Measure the length of the 5 remaining pieced bars through the center. Each pieced bar will measure 36½" long (raw edge to raw edge) if stitched perfectly. However, your bars may be a little longer or shorter. If the bars measure different lengths, determine the average length.

2. Cut the 38"-long blue-and-gray plaid strips to the length determined in step 1.

3. Join the pieced bars and the plaid strips along the long edges as shown. If you used the average bar measurement, you can take care of any minor discrepancies by easing either the pieced bars or the plaid strips as you sew. Press the seams toward the plaid strips.

   Measure the width of the quilt through the center. Cut the 4"-wide pieced bars the width measured and join them to the top and bottom edges of the quilt, matching ends and centers and easing as necessary. Press the seams however you wish.

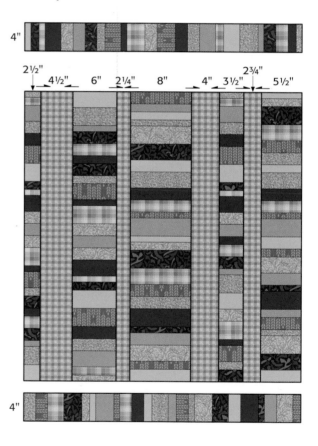

4. Join the borders to the quilt (see "Borders with Straight-Cut Corners" on pages 18–19). For the inner border, measure the length of the quilt through the center. Cut 2 of the 3½"-wide blue-and-gray plaid strips to the length measured and join them to the sides of the

quilt, matching the ends and centers and easing as necessary; press the seams toward the borders. Measure the width of the quilt through the center, including the border pieces you just added. Cut 2 blue-and-gray plaid border strips to the width measured and join them to the top and bottom of the quilt; press the seams toward the borders.

5. For the outer border, seam the 4"-wide dark blue print strips as necessary to make strips long enough to border the quilt; press the seams open. Measure the length of the quilt through the center. Cut 2 border strips to the length measured and join them to the sides of the quilt as above; press the seams toward the outer borders. Measure the width of the quilt through the center. Cut 2 border strips to the width measured and join them to the top and bottom of the quilt; press the seams toward the outer borders.

NOTE: *In the pictured quilt, the border width varies from edge to edge, probably because the pictured quilt is really the back side of Peter's actual quilt (!) and the size needed to be adjusted to fit the front. You can leave the outer border strips all the same width or trim the left side border to 2½", the right side border to 3½", and the bottom border to 3¼".*

Layering and Finishing the Quilt

1. Divide the backing fabric into 2 equal panels. Remove the selvages and join the panels with a ½" seam to make a single, large backing piece. Press the seam open.

2. Center the batting and quilt top on the backing; baste (see "Layering and Basting the Quilt" on pages 21–22).

3. Quilt or tack as desired (see "Quilting" on pages 22–25).

4. Bind the quilt with the 2½"-wide blue-and-gray plaid strips (see "Binding" on pages 26–28).

5. Make a label and stitch it to your quilt (see "Making a Label" on page 28).

DAISIES WON'T TELL

By Anne M. Richardson, 46" x 55". Quilted by Julie Kimberlin. The gray, yellow, and maroon floral print
set the color scheme for this quilt, which is enlivened by the narrow, striped inner border.

Finished Quilt Size: 46½" x 55½"

Materials

Yardage is based on 42"-wide fabric.

♦ 2 yds. of floral print for blocks, outer border, and binding
♦ ⅞ yd. of tan print for blocks
♦ ¾ yd. of pale yellow print for blocks
♦ ½ yd. of dark gray print for blocks
♦ ¼ yd. of rose stripe for inner border
♦ 3¼ yds. of fabric for backing (crosswise seam)
♦ 52" x 61" piece of batting

Cutting

All cutting measurements include ¼"-wide seam allowances.

From the floral print, cut:
♦ 9 selvage-to-selvage strips, 2" wide
♦ 6 selvage-to-selvage strips, 4½" wide
♦ 6 selvage-to-selvage strips, 2½" wide

From the dark gray print, cut:
♦ 6 selvage-to-selvage strips, 2" wide
♦ 1 square, 2" x 2"

From the pale yellow print, cut:
♦ 4 selvage-to-selvage strips, 5" wide; cut 2 strips into 40 rectangles, 2" x 5". Leave 2 strips uncut.

From the tan print, cut:
♦ 3 selvage-to-selvage strips, 8" wide; cut 1 strip into 20 rectangles, 2" x 8". Leave 2 strips uncut.

From the rose stripe, cut:
♦ 5 selvage-to-selvage strips, 1" wide

Making the Blocks

1. Join 2"-wide floral print strips and 2"-wide dark gray strips to make 2 strip unit A and 1 strip unit B as shown. Press the seams toward the dark gray strips. The strip units should measure 5" wide (raw edge to raw edge) when sewn. From each strip unit, cut the number of 2"-wide segments indicated below.

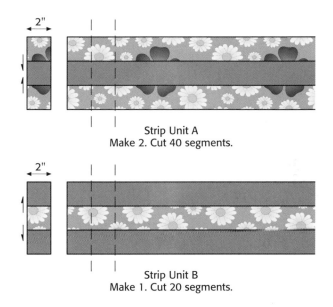

Strip Unit A
Make 2. Cut 40 segments.

Strip Unit B
Make 1. Cut 20 segments.

2. Join the segments from strip units A and B to make 20 Nine Patch blocks as shown. Press the seams however you wish. The Nine Patch blocks should measure 5" x 5" (raw edge to raw edge) when sewn.

Make 20.

3. Join 2" x 5" pale yellow rectangles to opposite sides of each Nine Patch block to make 20 units as shown. Press the seams toward the rectangles. The units should measure 5" x 8" (raw edge to raw edge) when sewn.

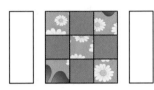 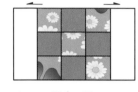

Make 20.

4. Join 2"-wide floral strips to each side of the 5"-wide pale yellow strips to make 2 strip unit C as shown. Press the seams toward the pale yellow print. The strip units should measure 8" wide (raw edge to raw edge) when sewn. From these strip units, cut a total of 40 segments, each 2" wide.

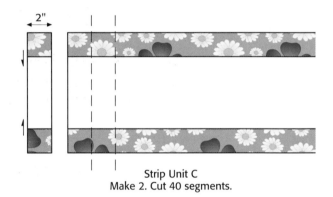

Strip Unit C
Make 2. Cut 40 segments.

5. Join segments from strip unit C to opposite sides of each unit from step 3 to make 20 units as shown. Press the seams however you wish. The units should measure 8" x 8" (raw edge to raw edge) when sewn.

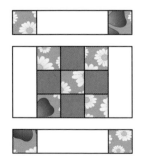 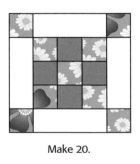

Make 20.

6. Join a 2" x 8" tan rectangle to one side of each of the units from step 5 to make 20 units as shown. Press the seams toward the tan rectangles. The units should measure 9½" x 8" (raw edge to raw edge) when sewn.

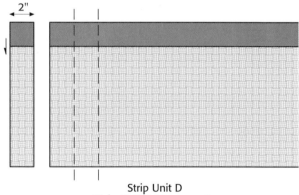

Make 20.

7. Join 2"-wide dark gray strips to 8"-wide tan strips to make 2 strip unit D as shown. Press the seams toward the tan strip. The strip units should measure 9½" wide (raw edge to raw edge) when sewn. From these strip units, cut a total of 29 segments, each 2" wide.

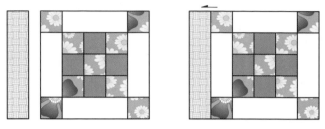

Strip Unit D
Make 2. Cut 29 segments.

8. Join a strip unit D segment to each unit from step 6 to make 20 blocks as shown. Press the seams however you wish. The blocks should measure 9½" x 9½" (raw edge to raw edge) when sewn.

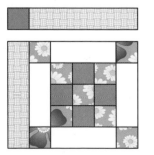 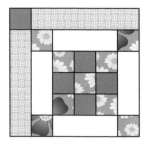

Make 20.

Assembling the Quilt Top

1. Join the blocks to make 5 horizontal rows of 4 blocks each as shown. Press the seams in opposite directions from row to row. Stitch the rows together. Press the seams in one direction.

2. Join 4 of the remaining segments from strip unit D end to end to make the bottom sashing strip as shown; stitch this pieced strip to the bottom edge of the quilt. Press the seam in the same direction as the other rows.

3. Join the remaining 5 segments from strip unit D and the 2" dark gray square end to end to make the sashing strip for the right side of the quilt as shown; stitch this pieced strip to the right side of the quilt. Press the seam however you wish.

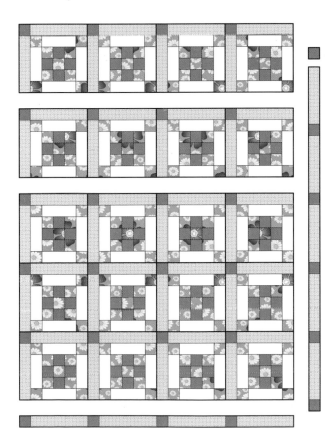

4. Join the borders to the quilt (see "Borders with Straight-Cut Corners" on pages 18–19). For the inner border, seam the 1"-wide rose stripe strips as necessary to make strips long enough to border the quilt; press the seams open. Measure the length of the quilt through the center. Cut 2 border strips to the length measured and join them to the sides of the quilt, matching the ends and centers and easing as necessary; press the seams toward the borders. Measure the width of the quilt through the center, including the border pieces you just added. Cut 2 border strips to the width measured and join them to the top and bottom of the quilt; press the seams toward the borders. Repeat with the 4½"-wide floral print strips for the outer border.

Layering and Finishing the Quilt

1. Divide the backing fabric into 2 equal panels. Remove the selvages and join the panels with a ½" seam to make a single, large backing piece. Press the seam open.

2. Center the batting and quilt top on the backing; baste (see "Layering and Basting the Quilt" on pages 21–22).

3. Quilt or tack as desired (see "Quilting" on pages 22–25).

4. Bind the quilt with the 2½"-wide floral print strips (see "Binding" on pages 26–28).

5. Make a label and stitch it to your quilt (see "Making a Label" on page 28).

JAPANESE SAMPLER

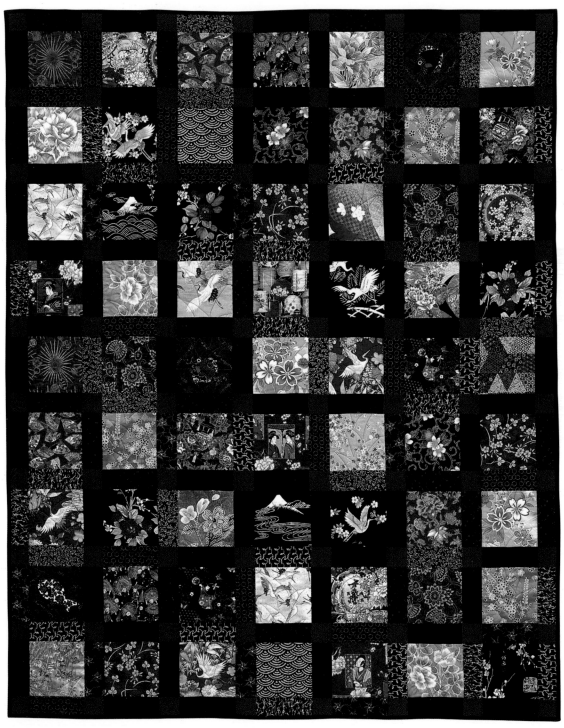

By Judy Forrest, 54" x 69". Quilted by Sandi Fruehling. This very simple design is the perfect setting for Judy's collection of elegant Japanese prints. The bright red sashing squares are an important unifying element.

Finished Quilt Size: 54½" x 69½"

Materials

Yardage is based on 42"-wide fabric.

- 1 fat quarter *each* of 9 assorted white-on-black and black-on-black prints for sashing strips
- 63 squares, 6" x 6", of assorted Japanese-style prints for blocks★
- ½ yd. of red print for sashing squares
- 4 yds. of fabric for backing (crosswise seam)
- ⅝ yd. of black fabric for binding
- 60" x 75" piece of batting

★*Use the same fabric more than once if you wish.*

Use an assortment of fabrics for the sashing strips.

Cutting

All cutting measurements include ¼"-wide seam allowances.

From each of the 9 fat quarters, cut:
- 2 strips, 6" x 21"★★ (18 total); cut the strips into 2½"-wide segments to make a total of 142 rectangles, 2½" x 6"

From the red print, cut:
- 5 selvage-to-selvage strips, 2½" wide; cross-cut the strips to make a total of 80 squares, 2½" x 2½"

From the black fabric, cut:
- 7 selvage-to-selvage strips, 2½" wide

★★*Because the size of fat quarters can vary, the strip length (21") is approximate. Cut the strips the full length of the longest side of the fat quarter.*

Assembling the Quilt Top

Because there are so many different fabric combinations, strip-piecing methods are not efficient for this quilt.

1. For the block rows, alternately join 8 sashing strips and 7 Japanese-print squares to make 9 rows as shown; combine the fabrics at random. Press the seams toward the sashing strips.

Make 9.

2. For the sashing rows, alternately join 8 red sashing squares and 7 sashing strips to make 10 rows as shown; combine the fabrics at random. Press the seams toward the sashing strips.

Make 10.

3. Join the block and sashing rows as shown. Press the seams however you wish.

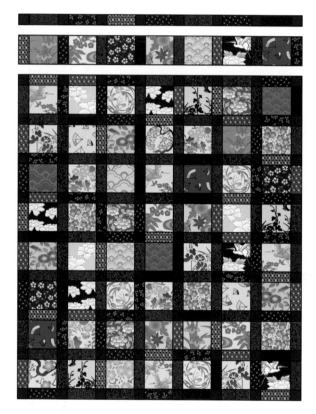

Layering and Finishing the Quilt

1. Divide the backing fabric into 2 equal panels. Remove the selvages and join the panels with a ½" seam to make a single, large backing piece. Press the seam open.

2. Center the batting and quilt top on the backing; baste (see "Layering and Basting the Quilt" on pages 21–22).

3. Quilt or tack as desired (see "Quilting" on pages 22–25).

4. Bind the quilt with the 2½"-wide black strips (see "Binding" on pages 26–28).

5. Make a label and stitch it to your quilt (see "Making a Label" on page 28).

Creative Options

THIS SIMPLE design is perfect for showcasing any special collection of fabrics. Try it in cheerful juvenile prints, with bright crayon colors for the sashing. If you use two patches each from many different prints, your cozy kids' quilt will be a fun matching game, too!

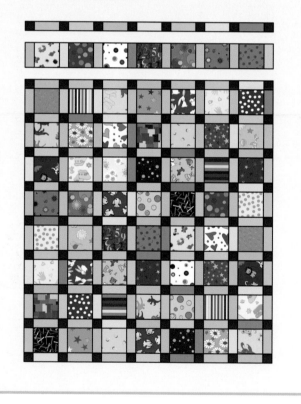

SANTA BARBARA BREEZES

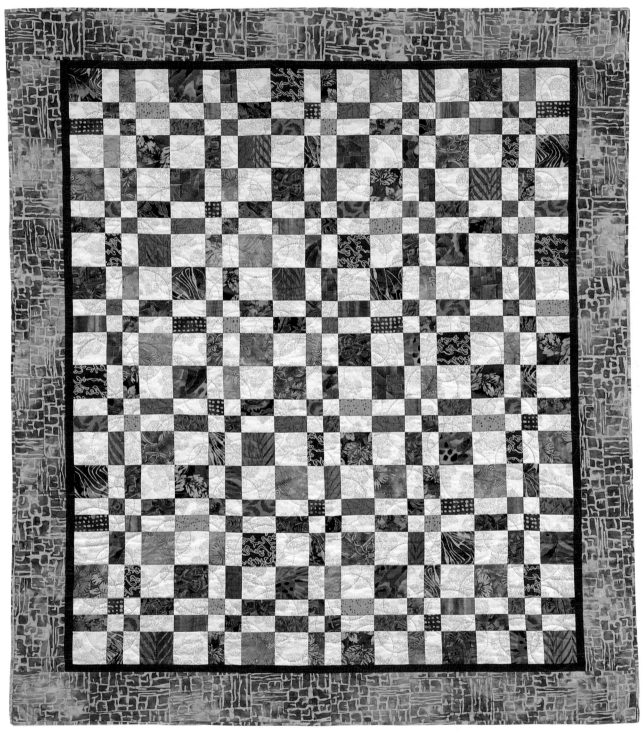

By Julie Wilkinson Kimberlin, 55" x 64". Julie has a special interest in batik fabrics. This easy counterchange design makes the most of the blue, turquoise, and purple batiks in her collection.

Finished Quilt Size: 57" x 66"

Materials

Yardage is based on 42"-wide fabric.

- 1⅞ yds. of turquoise print for outer border and binding
- 1⅝ yds. of light print for background
- 1 strip, exactly 3½" wide x about 42" long, *each* of 9 assorted turquoise and/or purple prints for blocks
- 1 strip, exactly 2" wide x about 42" long, *each* of 9 *different* turquoise and/or purple prints for blocks
- ⅜ yd. of deep purple stripe for inner border
- 4 yds. of fabric for backing (crosswise seam)
- 63" x 72" piece of batting

Cutting

All cutting measurements include ¼"-wide seam allowances.

From the light print, cut:
- 9 selvage-to-selvage strips, 3½" wide
- 9 selvage-to-selvage strips, 2" wide

From the deep purple stripe, cut:
- 7 selvage-to-selvage strips, 1¼" wide

From the turquoise print for outer border and binding, cut:
- 7 selvage-to-selvage strips, 5¾" wide
- 7 selvage-to-selvage strips, 2½" wide

Making the Blocks

THIS IS one of those designs that creates an occasional pressing conundrum no matter what you do. If you press the seams open, you may have difficulty matching seams, and you'll have no "ditch" to stitch in when you reach the quilting stage. If you press to the side, you may have to twist some seams

on the back when you assemble the blocks and/or the quilt, to make them butt together properly for easy joining.

1. Join the 3½"-wide light print strips, the 3½"-wide turquoise and/or purple print strips, the 2"-wide light print strips, and the 2"-wide turquoise and/or purple print strips to make 9 strip units as shown. Combine the turquoise and/or purple strips at random. Press the seams open or toward the darker strips. The strip units should measure 9½" wide (raw edge to raw edge) when sewn.

   From each strip unit, cut 7 segments, 3½" wide (63 total), and 7 segments, 2" wide (63 total). You will use 60 of each width and have 3 of each width left over.

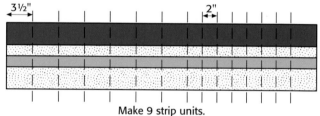

Make 9 strip units.
From each strip unit, cut seven 3¼"-wide segments (63 total) and seven 2"-wide segments (63 total).

2. Join the 3½"- and 2"-wide segments to make 60 units as shown, combining the fabrics at random. Press the seams open or toward the wider segments. The units should measure 5" x 9½" (raw edge to raw edge) when sewn.

Make 60.

3. Join the units from step 2 to make 30 blocks as shown, combining the fabrics at random. Press the seams open or to one side. The blocks should measure 9½" x 9½" (raw edge to raw edge) when sewn.

Make 30.

Assembling the Quilt Top

1. Join the blocks to make 6 rows of 5 blocks each as shown, positioning the blocks so the turquoise or purple corners are at the upper left and lower right. Press the seams in opposite directions from row to row. Join the rows. Press the seams in one direction.

2. Join the borders to the quilt (see "Borders with Straight-Cut Corners" on pages 18–19). For the inner border, seam the deep purple strips as necessary to make strips long enough to border the quilt; press the seams open. Measure the length of the quilt through the center. Cut 2 border strips to the length measured and join them to the sides of the quilt, matching the ends and centers and easing as necessary; press the seams toward the borders. Measure the width of the quilt through the center, including the border pieces you just added. Cut 2 border strips to the width measured and join them to the top and bottom of the quilt; press the seams toward the borders. Repeat with the 5¾"-wide turquoise strips for the outer border.

Layering and Finishing the Quilt

1. Divide the backing fabric into 2 equal panels. Remove the selvages and join the panels with a ½" seam to make a single, large backing piece. Press the seam open.

2. Center the batting and quilt top on the backing; baste (see "Layering and Basting the Quilt" on pages 21–22).

3. Quilt or tack as desired (see "Quilting" on pages 22–25).

4. Bind the quilt with the 2½"-wide turquoise print strips (see "Binding" on pages 26–28).

5. Make a label and stitch it to your quilt (see "Making a Label" on page 28).

Boxed In

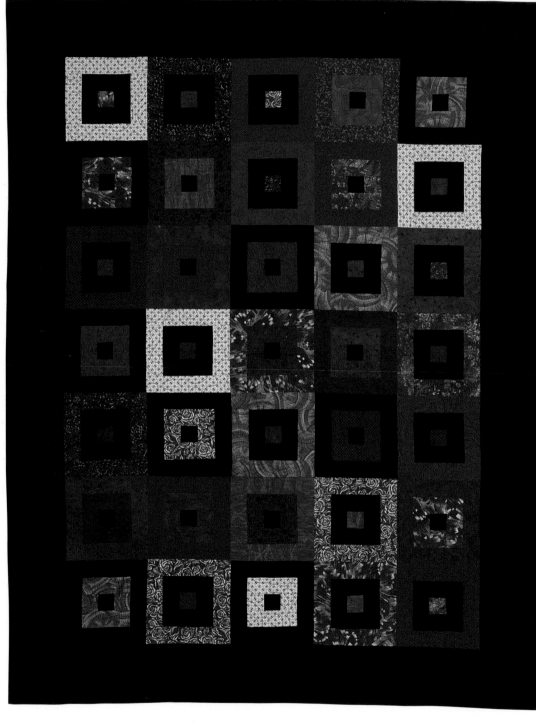

By Ann Liburd, 56" x 73½". Quilted by Bobbie Moore. This colorful concoction is Ann's second quilt.
The black fabric is the wrong side of a gray-on-black print.

Finished Quilt Size: 55¾" x 73¼"

Materials

Yardage is based on 42"-wide fabric.

♦ 3 yds. of black print or solid for blocks, border, and binding
♦ 1 fat quarter of light print for blocks
♦ 1 fat quarter of bright blue print for blocks
♦ 8" x 20" strip *each* of 17 assorted red prints for blocks
♦ 5" x 20" strip *each* of 5 *different* red prints for blocks
♦ 4 yds. of fabric for backing (crosswise seam)
♦ 62" x 79" piece of batting

Cutting

All cutting measurements include ¼"-wide seam allowances.

From the black print or solid, cut:
♦ 16 selvage-to-selvage strips, 2¼" wide; crosscut the strips to make:
  • 16 strips, 2¼" x 9¼"
  • 50 strips, 2¼" x 5¾"
  • 52 squares, 2¼" x 2¼"
♦ 7 selvage-to-selvage strips, 6½" wide
♦ 7 selvage-to-selvage strips, 2½" wide

From the light print, cut:
♦ 6 strips, 2¼" x 21"*; crosscut the strips to make:
  • 6 strips, 2¼" x 9¼"
  • 8 strips, 2¼" x 5¾"
  • 2 squares, 2¼" x 2¼"

From the bright blue print, cut:
♦ 6 strips, 2¼" x 21"*; crosscut the strips to make:
  • 4 strips, 2¼" x 9¼"
  • 8 strips, 2¼" x 5¾"
  • 4 squares, 2¼" x 2¼"

From *each* of the 8" x 20" red print strips, cut:
♦ 3 strips, 2¼" x 20"; from each set of 3 matching strips, cut:
  • 2 strips, 2¼" x 9¼" (34 total)
  • 4 strips, 2¼" x 5¾" (68 total; you will use 64 and have 4 left over)
  • 3 squares, 2¼" x 2¼" (51 total; you will use 47 and have 4 left over)

From *each* of the 5" x 20" red print strips, cut:
♦ 2 strips, 2¼" x 20"; from each matching pair of strips, cut:
  • 2 strips, 2¼" x 9¼" (10 total)
  • 2 strips, 2¼" x 5¾" (10 total)

*Because the size of fat quarters can vary, the strip length (21") is approximate. Cut the strips the full length of the longest side of the fat quarter.

Making the Blocks

BECAUSE THERE are so many different fabric combinations, strip-piecing methods are not efficient for this quilt.

1. Join 2¼" black squares and 2¼" x 5¾" black strips to 17 of the red squares as shown. Use a different red print in each unit. Press the seams toward the black pieces. The units should measure 5¾" x 5¾" (raw edge to raw edge) when sewn.

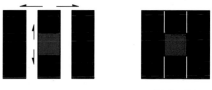

Make 17.

2. Join 2¼" x 5¾" blue strips and 2¼" x 9¼" blue strips to 2 of the units from step 1 as shown on page 74. Press the seams toward the blue strips.

   To 3 of the units from step 1, join 2¼" x 5¾" light strips and 2¼" x 9¼" light strips as shown below. Press the seams toward the light strips.

Using matching red strips, join 2¼" x 5¾" and 2¼" x 9¼" strips to the 12 remaining units from step 1 as shown. The red print used for the outside of a block should be different from the red used for that block's center square. Press the seams toward the red strips. The blocks should measure 9¼" x 9¼" (raw edge to raw edge) when sewn.

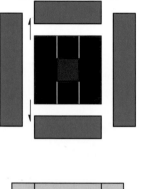

Make 2.

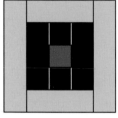

Make 3.

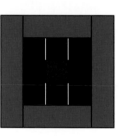

Make 12.

3. Using matching red pieces, join 2¼" squares and 2¼" x 5¾" strips to fifteen 2¼" black squares as shown. Press the seams toward the red strips.

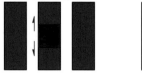

Make 15.

Join 2¼" blue squares and 2¼" x 5¾" blue strips to two 2¼" black squares as shown. Press the seams toward the blue strips.

Make 2.

Join 2¼" light squares and 2¼" x 5¾" light strips to a 2¼" black square as shown. Press

the seams toward the light strips.

All the units should measure 5¾" x 5¾" (raw edge to raw edge) when sewn.

Make 1.

4. Using matching red strips, join 2¼" x 5¾" strips and 2¼" x 9¼" strips to 10 of the red units from step 3 as shown. The red print used for the outside of the block should be different from the red print used for the inside of the block. Press the seams toward the outer red strips. The blocks should measure 9¼" x 9¼" (raw edge to raw edge) when sewn.

Make 10.

5. Join 2¼" x 5¾" and 2¼" x 9¼" black strips to the remaining 8 units from step 3 as shown. Press the seams toward the black strips. The blocks should measure 9¼" x 9¼" (raw edge to raw edge) when sewn.

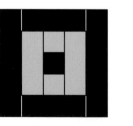

Make 1.

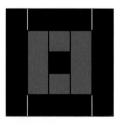

Make 2.

Make 5.

Assembling the Quilt Top

1. Join the blocks to make 7 horizontal rows of 5 blocks each, referring to the quilt photo for block placement. Rotate every other block as shown to avoid having to match more seams than necessary. Press the seams in opposite directions from row to row. Join the rows. Press the seams in one direction.

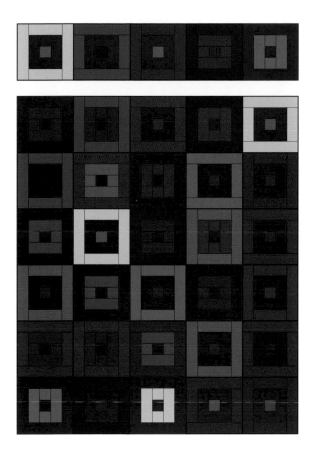

2. Join the border to the quilt (see "Borders with Straight-Cut Corners" on pages 18–19): Seam the 6½"-wide black strips as necessary to make strips long enough to border the quilt; press the seams open. Measure the length of the quilt through the center. Cut 2 border strips to the length measured and join them to the sides of the quilt, matching the ends and centers and easing as necessary; press the seams toward the borders. Measure the width of the quilt through the center, including the border pieces you just added. Cut 2 border strips to the width measured and join them to the top and bottom of the quilt; press the seams toward the borders.

Layering and Finishing the Quilt

1. Divide the backing fabric into 2 equal panels. Remove the selvages and join the panels with a ½" seam to make a single, large backing piece. Press the seam open.

2. Center the batting and quilt top on the backing; baste (see "Layering and Basting the Quilt" on pages 21–22).

3. Quilt or tack as desired (see "Quilting" on pages 22–25).

4. Bind the quilt with the 2½"-wide black strips (see "Binding" on pages 26–28).

5. Make a label and stitch it to your quilt (see "Making a Label" on page 28).

ARCTIC NIGHTS

By Judy Dafoe Hopkins, 56¾" x 73". Quilted by Barbara Ford. Made to showcase Marsha McCloskey's first fabric line, this quilt also sports an abundance of green and blue-green fabrics from my stash.

Finished Quilt Size: 60" x 76"

Materials

Yardage is based on 42"-wide fabric.

- ◆ 1 strip, exactly 2½" wide x about 42" long, *each* of 32 assorted light prints for blocks*
- ◆ 1 strip, exactly 2½" wide x about 42" long, *each* of 32 assorted dark blue, blue-green, and green prints for blocks**
- ◆ 1 strip, exactly 6½" wide x about 42" long, *each* of 7 assorted light prints for pieced border
- ◆ 5 yds. of fabric for backing (lengthwise seam)
- ◆ ¾ yd. of green print for binding
- ◆ 66" x 82" piece of batting

Use the same fabric more than once if you wish. For instance, you could use 4 different light prints and cut 8 strips, 2½" x 42", from each one (purchase ¾ yard of each). Or you could use 8 different light prints and cut 4 strips, 2½" x 42", from each one (purchase ⅜ yard of each).

**Use the same fabric more than once if you wish, but use at least 8 different prints. If you use 8 prints, cut 4 strips, 2½" x 42", from each (purchase ⅜ yard of each). If you use 16 prints, cut 2 strips, 2½" x 42", from each (purchase ¼ yard of each).*

Cutting

All cutting measurements include ¼"-wide seam allowances.

From the green print for binding, cut:
- ◆ 8 selvage-to-selvage strips, 2½" wide

Making the Blocks

THIS IS one of those designs that creates an occasional pressing conundrum no matter what you do. If you press the seams open, you may have difficulty matching seam, and you'll have no "ditch" to stitch in when you reach the quilting stage. If you press to the side, you may have to twist some seams on the back when you assemble the blocks and/or the quilt, to make them butt together properly for easy joining.

1. Layer a 2½"-wide light strip and a 2½"-wide dark strip *right sides together*. Keep the long edges aligned. Square up one end of this layered strip pair, then cut: 3 rectangles, 2½" x 4½" (A), 3 squares, 2½" x 2½" (B), and 3 rectangles, 1½" x 2½" (C). Set these pieces aside for now.

Place right sides together.

2. From the remaining piece of the layered strip pair, cut 1 strip, 1½" by about 11", as shown.

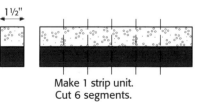

3. Seam the 1½" x 11" layered strip along the long edge to make a strip unit. Press the seam open or toward the darker fabric. The strip unit should measure 2½" wide (raw edge to raw edge) when sewn. From this strip unit, cut a total of 6 segments, 1½" wide.

Make 1 strip unit.
Cut 6 segments.

4. Join a strip-unit segment from step 3 to each of the C rectangles from step 1 as shown, being careful to orient the strip-unit segments in the correct direction in each combination. Make 3 of each combination. Press the seams open or in the direction indicated. The units should measure 2½" x 2½" (raw edge to raw edge) when sewn.

Make 3.   Make 3.

5. Join the B squares from step 1 to the units from step 4 as shown, being careful to add the correct light or dark square to the unit indicated. Make 3 of each combination. Press the seams open or in the direction indicated. The units should measure 2½" x 4½" (raw edge to raw edge) when sewn.

Make 3.   Make 3.

6. Stitch the A rectangles from step 1 to the units from step 5 as shown, being careful to add the correct light or dark rectangle to the unit indicated. Make 3 dark units and 3 light units. Press the seams open or in the direction indicated. The units should measure 4½" x 4½" (raw edge to raw edge) when sewn.

Dark Unit   Light Unit
Make 3.   Make 3.

7. Repeat steps 1–6 with the remaining 2½"-wide light strips and the remaining 2½"-wide dark strips. Now that you know what you're doing, you can work with several layered strip pairs at once if you wish. Just remember that the finished units should each contain just 2 fabrics—1 light and 1 dark. When you have cut and stitched all 32 sets of strips, you will have 96 light units and 96 dark units (192 total).

8. Randomly join 2 light units and 2 dark units to make 48 blocks as shown. Press the seams however you wish. The blocks should measure 8½" x 8½" (raw edge to raw edge) when sewn.

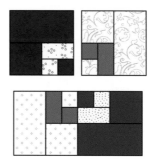 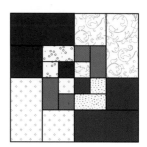

Make 48.

Assembling the Quilt Top

1. Join the blocks to make 8 horizontal rows of 6 blocks each as shown on the facing page. Note that the blocks should be arranged so that blue, blue-green, or green corners appear at the upper left and lower right. Press the seams in opposite directions from row to row. Join the rows. Press the seams in one direction.

2. From the 6½"-wide light print strips, cut 17 segments 12½" long (A), 3 segments 10½" long (B), and 1 segment 14½" long (C).

3. Join the border pieces end to end to make 4 pieced border strips as shown. Attach the border strips to the bottom edge of the quilt, then the sides, and finally the top edge. Press the seams toward the border strip after each addition.

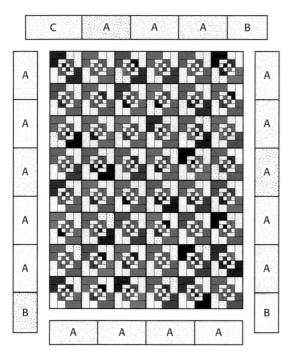

Layering and Finishing the Quilt

1. Divide the backing fabric into 2 equal panels. Remove the selvages and join the panels with a ½" seam to make a single, large backing piece. Press the seam open.

2. Center the batting and quilt top on the backing; baste (see "Layering and Basting the Quilt" on pages 21–22).

3. Quilt or tack as desired (see "Quilting" on pages 22–25).

4. Bind the quilt with the 2½"-wide green print binding strips (see "Binding" on pages 26–28).

5. Make a label and stitch it to your quilt (see "Making a Label" on page 28).

Creative Options

IN POSITIVE-NEGATIVE (or "counter-change") designs, the light and dark areas reverse from block to block (or from quadrant to quadrant within the block, as with Arctic Nights). Positive-negative designs always work well for scrappy-looking quilts, and they're an excellent choice for two-fabric quilts as well. For example, the Arctic Nights block would be terrific made up in muslin and a red solid, as shown, or in a single light print and a single dark print.

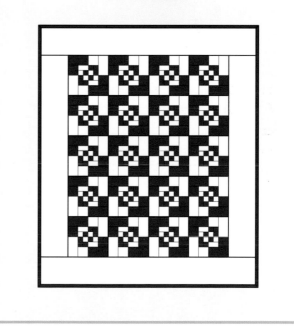

STRIP STACCATO

By Judy Dafoe Hopkins, 55¼" x 70¼". Quilted by Becky Crook.
The blue-violet fabrics are lovely, but it's the white-hot nine-patches that make this quilt sing.

Finished Quilt Size: 57¾" x 72¾"

Materials

Yardage is based on 42"-wide fabric. Paste a snip of each medium and dark blue-violet print to an index card and label the strips for reference during the cutting-and-assembling process.

- ⅜ yd. of light print for Nine Patch blocks
- ⅝ yd. of hot pink print for Nine Patch blocks and inner border
- ½ yd. of medium blue-violet print 1 (medium 1) for strip units
- 2¼ yds. of medium blue-violet print 2 (medium 2) for strip units and outer border
- ½ yd. of medium blue-violet print 3 (medium 3) for strip units
- ½ yd. of dark blue-violet print 1 (dark 1) for strip units
- ½ yd. of dark blue-violet print 2 (dark 2) for strip units
- 1 yd. of dark blue-violet print 3 (dark 3) for strip units and binding
- 4 yds. of fabric for backing (crosswise seam)
- 64" x 79" piece of batting

Cutting

All cutting measurements include ¼"-wide seam allowances.

From the light print, cut:
- 4 selvage-to-selvage strips, 1¾" wide

From the hot pink print, cut:
- 5 selvage-to-selvage strips, 1¾" wide
- 6 selvage-to-selvage strips, 1" wide

From *each* medium 1, dark 1, and dark 2 print, cut:
- 8 selvage-to-selvage strips, 1¾" wide (24 total)

From *each* medium 2, medium 3, and dark 3 print, cut:
- 7 selvage-to-selvage strips, 1¾" wide (21 total)

From the remaining piece of medium 2 print, cut:
- 7 selvage-to-selvage strips, 8¼" wide

From the remaining piece of dark 3 print, cut:
- 7 selvage-to-selvage strips, 2½" wide

Making the Blocks and Assembling the Quilt Top

1. Join 1¾"-wide hot pink strips and 1¾"-wide light strips to make 2 strip unit A and 1 strip unit B as shown. Press the seams toward the hot pink strips. The strip units should measure 4¼" wide (raw edge to raw edge) when sewn. Cut the number of 1¾"-wide segments indicated below from each strip unit.

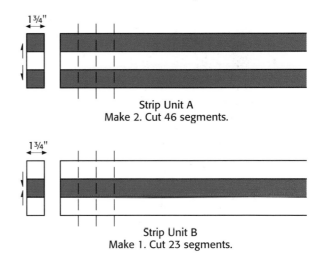

Strip Unit A
Make 2. Cut 46 segments.

Strip Unit B
Make 1. Cut 23 segments.

2. Join the segments from strip units A and B to make 23 Nine Patch blocks as shown. Press the seams however you wish. The blocks should measure 4¼" x 4¼" (raw edge to raw edge) when sewn.

Make 23.

3. Join 1¾"-wide dark 1, medium 1, and dark 2 strips to make 8 strip units as shown. Press the seams toward the medium 1 strips. The strip units should measure 4¼" wide (raw edge to raw edge) when sewn.

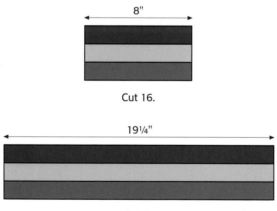

Dark 1
Medium 1
Dark 2

Make 8.

4. From 4 of the strip units you made in step 3, cut a total of 16 segments, each 8" wide. From the remaining 4 strip units, cut a total of 8 segments, each 19¼" wide.

8"

Cut 16.

19¼"

Cut 8.

5. Join the Nine Patch blocks and the segments from step 4 to make 8 rows as shown. Press the seams however you wish.

Make 8.

6. Join the 1¾"-wide medium 2, dark 3, and medium 3 strips to make 7 strip units as shown. Press the seams toward the dark 3 strip. The strip units should measure 4¼" wide (raw edge to raw edge) when sewn. From these strip units, cut a total of 14 segments, each 19¼" wide.

19¼"

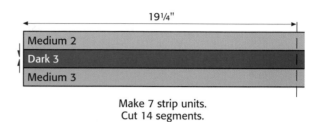

Medium 2
Dark 3
Medium 3

Make 7 strip units.
Cut 14 segments.

7. Join the segments from step 6 and the remaining Nine Patch blocks to make 7 rows as shown. Press the seams however you wish.

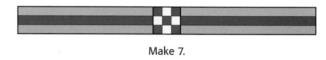

Make 7.

8. Alternately arrange the rows from steps 5 and 7 as shown. Join the rows. Press the seams however you wish.

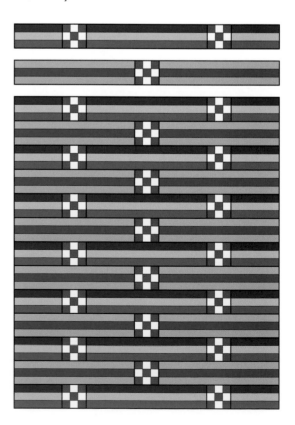

9. Join the borders to the quilt (see "Borders with Straight-Cut Corners" on page 18). For the inner border, seam the 1"-wide hot pink strips as necessary to make strips long enough to border the quilt; press the seams open. Measure the length of the quilt through the center. Cut 2 border strips to the length measured and join them to the sides of the quilt, matching the ends and centers and easing as necessary; press the seams toward the borders. Measure the width of the quilt through the center, including the border pieces you just added. Cut 2 border strips to the width measured and join them to the top and bottom of the quilt; press the seams toward the borders. Repeat with the 8¼"-wide medium 2 print strips for the outer border.

Layering and Finishing the Quilt

1. Divide the backing fabric into 2 equal panels. Remove the selvages and join the panels with a ½" seam to make a single, large backing piece. Press the seam open.

2. Center the batting and quilt top on the backing; baste (see "Layering and Basting the Quilt" on pages 21–22).

3. Quilt or tack as desired (see "Quilting" on pages 22–25).

4. Bind the quilt with the 2½"-wide dark 3 print strips (see "Binding" on pages 26–28).

5. Make a label and stitch it to your quilt (see "Making a Label" on page 28).

Tip

LIGHT-TO-DARK value gradations work well in blocks or quilts that contain stacks of strips. "Strip Staccato," for instance, could be made with six prints or solids that grade from very light to very dark, all the same color or different colors, arranged as shown.

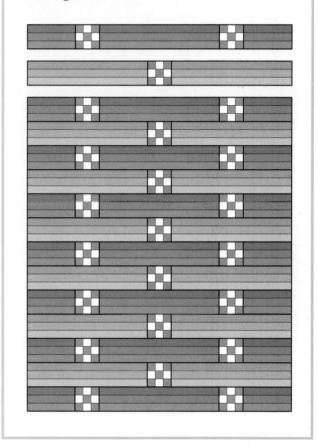

SPRUCE ROOT BASKET

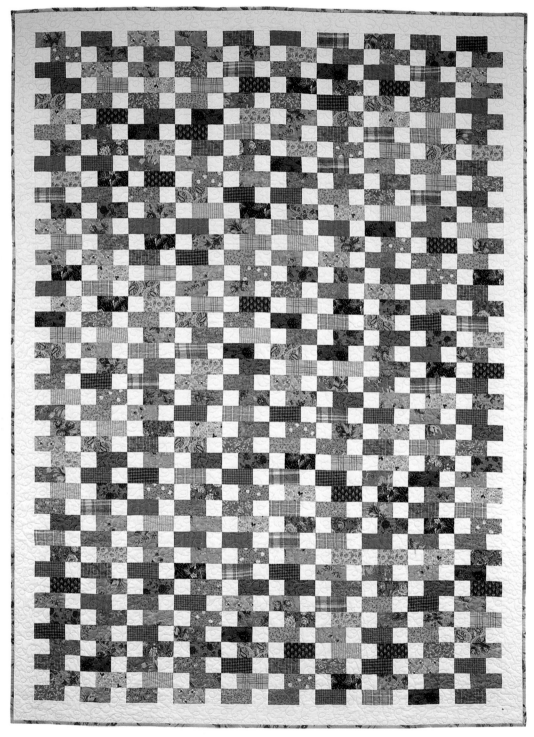

By Judy Dafoe Hopkins, 64¾" x 90". Quilted by Julie Fugate. A quilt-shop bundle of romantic pastels sets the tone for this quiet quilt.

Finished Quilt Size: 66" x 92"

Materials

Yardage is based on 42"-wide fabric.

- 3 yds. of muslin for blocks and border
- 14 strips, exactly 4½" wide and about 42" long, of assorted pastel blue and pastel green prints for blocks★
- 14 strips, exactly 4½" wide and about 42" long, of assorted pastel yellow and pastel orchid prints for blocks★
- 6 yds. of fabric for backing (lengthwise seam)
- ¾ yd. of pastel print for binding
- 72" x 98" piece of batting

★*Use the same fabric more than once if you wish.*

Cutting

All cutting measurements include ¼"-wide seam allowances.

From the muslin, cut:
- 28 selvage-to-selvage strips, 2½" wide
- 9 selvage-to-selvage strips, 3½" wide

From the pastel print for binding, cut:
- 9 selvage-to-selvage strips, 2½" wide

Assembling the Quilt Top

1. Join 2½"-wide muslin strips to the 4½"-wide blue and green strips to make 14 strip unit A as shown. Press the seams toward the pastel strips. The strip units should measure 6½" wide (raw edge to raw edge) when sewn. From these strip units, cut a total of 220 segments, each 2½" wide.

2½"

Strip Unit A
Make 14. Cut 220 segments.

2. Join 2½"-wide muslin strips to the 4½"-wide yellow and orchid strips to make 14 strip unit B as shown. Press the seams toward the pastel strips. The strip units should measure 6½" wide (raw edge to raw edge) when sewn. From these strip units, cut a total of 210 segments, each 2½" wide.

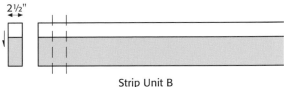

2½"

Strip Unit B
Make 14. Cut 210 segments.

3. Join 22 of the blue or green segments and 21 of the yellow or orchid segments vertically to make a row as shown. Note that the blue or green segments all appear on the left side of the row; the yellow or orchid segments all appear on the right. Repeat to make a total of 10 rows. Press the seams in opposite directions from row to row. Join the rows. Press the seams however you wish.

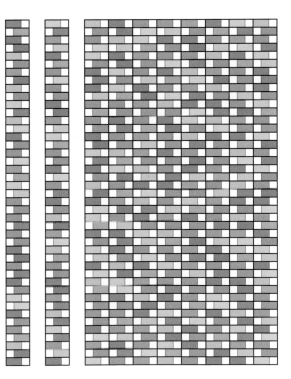

4. Join the border to the quilt (see "Borders with Straight-Cut Corners" on pages 18–19): Seam the 3½"-wide muslin strips as necessary to make strips long enough to border the quilt; press the seams open. Measure the length of the quilt through the center. Cut 2 border strips to the length measured and join them to the sides of the quilt, matching the ends and centers and easing as necessary; press the seams toward the borders. Measure the width of the quilt through the center, including the border pieces you just added. Cut 2 border strips to the width measured and join them to the top and bottom of the quilt; press the seams toward the borders.

Layering and Finishing the Quilt

1. Divide the backing fabric into 2 equal panels. Remove the selvages and join the panels with a ½" seam to make a single, large backing piece. Press the seam open.

2. Center the batting and quilt top on the backing; baste (see "Layering and Basting the Quilt" on pages 21–22).

3. Quilt or tack as desired (see "Quilting" on pages 22–25).

4. Bind the quilt with the 2½"-wide pastel print strips (see "Binding" on pages 26–28).

5. Make a label and stitch it to your quilt (see "Making a Label" on page 28).

Creative Options

BRICKLIKE QUILTS work up well in masculine colors and fabrics, too! Made up in sports prints or school colors as shown, "Spruce Root Basket" would be a good quilt for one of the men in your life.

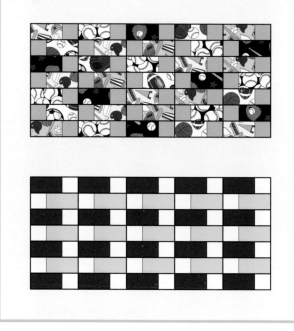

MIXING TRADITIONS

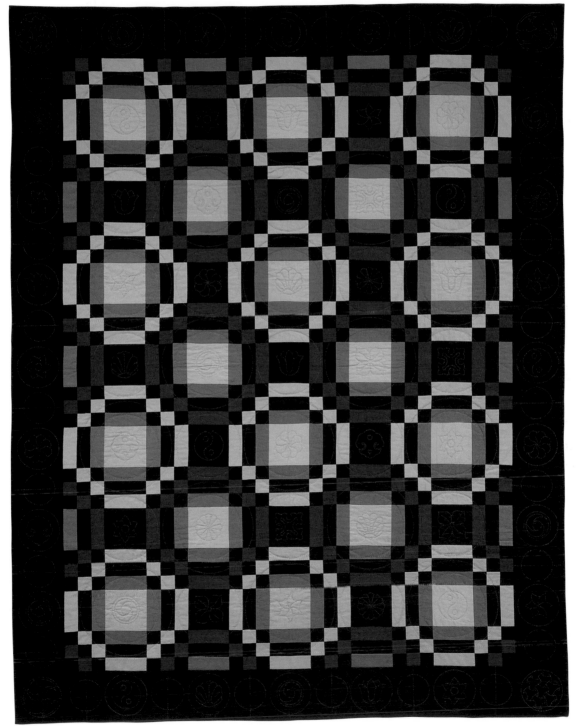

*By Julie Wilkinson Kimberlin, 60" x 78". Julie used Amish colors and lovely curvilinear
Japanese quilting designs for this quilt—thus "mixing traditions."*

Finished Quilt Size: 60½" x 78½"

Materials

Yardage is based on 42"-wide fabric. Paste snips of fabrics 1–5 to an index card and number the snips for reference during the cutting-and-assembling process.

- Fabric 1: ¾ yd. of medium blue solid for blocks
- Fabric 2: ¾ yd. of medium violet solid for blocks
- Fabric 3: ⅞ yd. of light blue solid for blocks
- Fabric 4: ⅝ yd. of light violet solid for blocks
- Fabric 5: 4⅛ yds. of black solid for blocks, border, and binding
- 5¼ yds. of fabric for backing (lengthwise seam)
- 66" x 84" piece of batting

Cutting

All cutting measurements include ¼"-wide seam allowances.

From fabric 1, cut:
- 11 selvage-to-selvage strips, 2" wide

From fabric 2, cut:
- 11 selvage-to-selvage strips, 2" wide

From fabric 3, cut:
- 12 selvage-to-selvage strips, 2" wide

From fabric 4, cut:
- 3 selvage-to-selvage strips, 5" wide; crosscut the strips to make 18 squares, 5" x 5".

From fabric 5, cut:
- 26 selvage-to-selvage strips, 2" wide
- 3 selvage-to-selvage strips, 5" wide; crosscut the strips to make 17 squares, 5" x 5".
- 8 selvage-to-selvage strips, 6" wide
- 8 selvage-to-selvage strips, 2½" wide

Making the Blocks

1. Join 2"-wide strips of fabrics 1, 3, and 5 to make 3 each of strip units A, B, and C as shown. Press the seams in the directions indicated for each strip unit. The strip units should measure 5" wide (raw edge to raw edge) when sewn. From each strip unit, cut 16 segments, 2" wide. When you have finished cutting all 9 strip units, you will have a total of 144 segments.

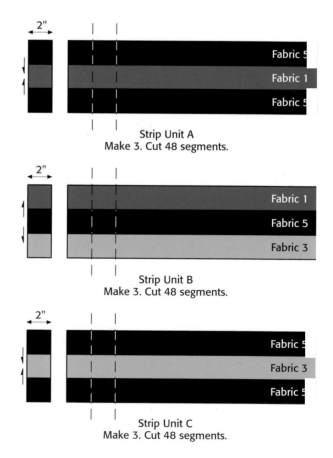

Strip Unit A
Make 3. Cut 48 segments.

Strip Unit B
Make 3. Cut 48 segments.

Strip Unit C
Make 3. Cut 48 segments.

2. Join segments from strip units A, B, and C to make 48 Block A as shown. Press the seams toward the center segments. The blocks should measure 5" x 5" (raw edge to raw edge) when sewn.

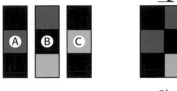

Block A
Make 48.

3. Join 2"-wide strips of fabrics 2, 3, and 5 to make 6 strip unit D as shown. Press the seams away from the center strips. The strip units should measure 5" wide (raw edge to raw edge) when sewn. Cut the strip units into 48 segments, 5" wide, to make Block B.

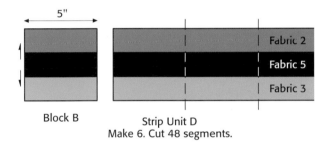

Block B

Strip Unit D
Make 6. Cut 48 segments.

4. Join 2"-wide strips of fabrics 1, 2, and 5 to make 5 strip unit E as shown. Press the seams away from the center strips. The strip units should measure 5" wide (raw edge to raw edge) when sewn. Cut the strip units into 34 segments, 5" wide, to make Block C.

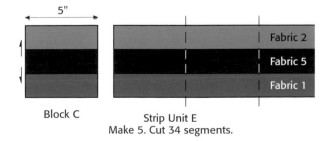

Block C

Strip Unit E
Make 5. Cut 34 segments.

Assembling the Quilt Top

1. Join Blocks A, B, and C and the 5" x 5" fabric 4 and 5 squares as shown to make 8 row 1, 4 row 2, and 3 row 3, paying careful attention to the orientation of each block in each row. Press the seams toward Blocks B and C.

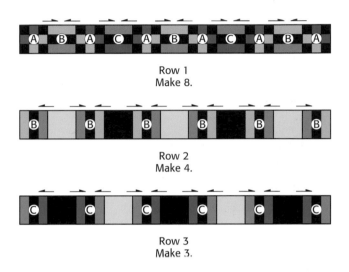

Row 1
Make 8.

Row 2
Make 4.

Row 3
Make 3.

2. Join the rows from step 1 as shown, turning the row 1 strips that are marked with an asterisk upside down. Press the seams in one direction.

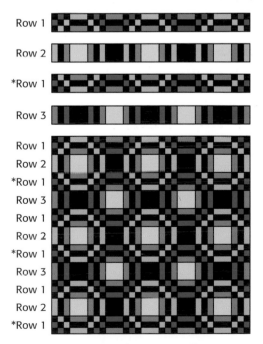

*Turn these row 1 strips upside down (rotate 180°).

3. Join the border to the quilt (see "Borders with Straight-Cut Corners" on page 18): Seam the 6"-wide fabric-5 strips as necessary to make strips long enough to border the quilt; press the seams open. Measure the length of the quilt through the center. Cut 2 border strips to the length measured and join them to the sides of the quilt, matching the ends and centers and easing as necessary. Press the seams toward the borders. Measure the width of the quilt through the center, including the border pieces you just added. Cut 2 border strips to the width measured and join them to the top and bottom of the quilt; press the seams toward the borders.

Layering and Finishing the Quilt

1. Divide the backing fabric into 2 equal panels. Remove the selvages and join the panels with a ½" seam to make a single, large backing piece. Press the seam open.

2. Center the batting and quilt top on the backing; baste (see "Layering and Basting the Quilt" on pages 21–22).

3. Quilt or tack as desired (see "Quilting" on pages 22–25).

4. Bind the quilt with the 2½"-wide fabric-5 strips (see "Binding" on pages 26–28).

5. Make a label and stitch it to your quilt (see "Making a Label" on page 28).

ILLUSIONS

By George Taylor, 77" x 96". This is not a restful quilt! It would be great on a conference
or classroom wall—no one would be inclined to sleep the afternoon away!

Finished Quilt Size: 78" x 97"

Materials

Yardage is based on 42"-wide fabric.

- 4¼ yds. of white-on-white print for blocks and middle border
- 4⅛ yds. of dark green solid for blocks, inner and outer borders, and binding
- 1½ yds. *each* of 2 different dark green solids, similar in value and hue to the green above, for blocks
- 7⅞ yds. of fabric for backing (2 crosswise seams)
- 84" x 103" piece of batting

NOTE: *George made his quilt with three subtly different dark green solids, and that is how the pattern is written, except that we've provided for a single-fabric border rather than a collaged border. If you want to use just one green fabric throughout, you'll need 6⅞ yards of a dark green solid for the blocks, inner and outer borders, and binding.*

Cutting

All cutting measurements include ¼"-wide seam allowances.

From the white-on-white print, cut:
- 55 selvage-to-selvage strips, 1½" wide
- 8 selvage-to-selvage strips, 2½" wide
- 6 selvage-to-selvage strips, 3½" wide
- 4 selvage-to-selvage strips, 4½" wide

From *each* of the 3 green solids, cut:
- 16 selvage-to-selvage strips, 1½" wide (48 total)
- 2 selvage-to-selvage strips, 2½" wide (6 total)
- 3 selvage-to-selvage strips, 3½" wide (9 total)
- 1 selvage-to-selvage strip, 4½" wide (3 total)

From the green solid for borders and binding, cut:
- 18 selvage-to-selvage strips, 2½" wide
- 9 selvage-to-selvage strips, 5½" wide

Making the Units

THIS IS ONE of those designs that creates an occasional pressing conundrum no matter what you do. I'd suggest pressing seams open throughout, but if you do, you may have difficulty matching seams, and you'll have no "ditch" to stitch in when you reach the quilting stage. If you press to the side, press toward the green fabrics when you make the strip units and press however you wish when you assemble the strip-unit segments you've cut. You may have to twist some seams on the back when you assemble the blocks and/or quilt to make them butt together properly for easy joining.

When constructing the units needed for this quilt, pick up and use the green strips at random.

1. Join 1½" white-on-white and green strips to make 9 strip units as shown. Press the seams toward the green fabrics. The strip units should measure 5½" wide (raw edge to raw edge) when sewn.

   From 3 of the strip units, cut a total of 60 segments, 1½" wide. Mark these "unit A" and set them aside. From the 6 remaining strip units, cut a total of 62 segments, 3½" wide. Mark these "unit B" and set them aside.

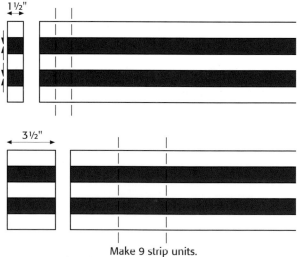

Make 9 strip units.
From 3 strip units, cut 60 segments, 1½" wide, for unit A.
From 6 strip units, cut 62 segments, 3½" wide, for unit B.

2. Join 1½" white-on-white and green strips to make 10 strip units as shown. Press the seams toward the green fabrics. The strip units should measure 5½" wide (raw edge to raw edge) when sewn.

   From 2 of the strip units, cut a total of 40 segments, 1½" wide. Mark these "unit A" and set them aside. From 4 of the strip units, cut a total of 62 segments, each 2½" wide. Mark these "unit B" and set them aside. From the remaining 4 strip units, cut 31 segments, 4½" wide. Mark these "unit B" and set them aside.

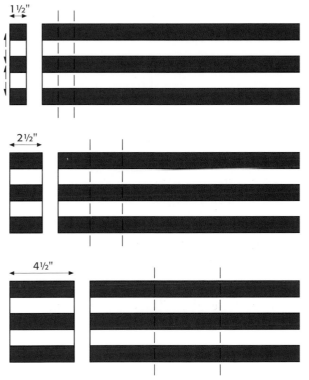

Make 10 strip units.
From 2 strip units, cut 40 segments, 1½" wide, for unit A.
From 4 strip units, cut 62 segments, 2½" wide, for unit B.
From 4 strip units, cut 31 segments, 4½" wide, for unit B.

3. Join the 1½"-wide unit A segments from steps 1 and 2 to make 20 unit A as shown. Combine the fabrics at random. Press the seams however you wish. The units should measure 5½" x 5½" (raw edge to raw edge) when sewn.

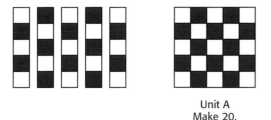

Unit A
Make 20.

4. Join the 2½"-, 3½"-, and 4½"-wide unit B segments from steps 1 and 2 to make 31 unit B as shown. Combine the fabrics at random. Press the seams however you wish. The units should measure 5½" x 14½" (raw edge to raw edge) when sewn.

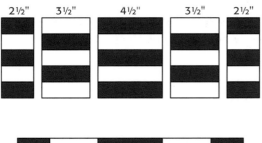

Unit B
Make 31.

5. Join 2½"- and 4½"-wide white-on-white strips and 3½"-wide green strips to make 4 strip units as shown. (You'll have one 3½"-wide green strip left over. Set it aside for another project.) Press the seams toward the green fabrics. The strip units should measure 14½" wide (raw edge to raw edge) when sewn.

   From 2 of the strip units, cut a total of 24 segments, 2½" wide. From the remaining 2 strip units, cut a total of 12 segments, 4½" wide.

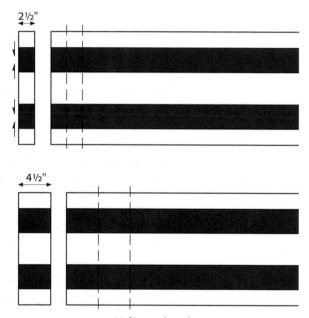

Make 4 strip units.
From 2 strip units, cut 24 segments, 2½" wide.
From 2 strip units, cut 12 segments, 4½" wide.

6. Join 3½"-wide white-on-white strips and 2½"- and 4½"-wide green strips to make 3 strip units as shown. Press the seams toward the green fabrics. The strip units should measure 14½" wide (raw edge to raw edge) when sewn.

   From the strip units, cut a total of 24 segments, 3½" wide.

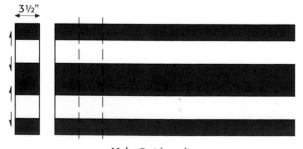

Make 3 strip units.
Cut 24 segments.

7. Join the 2½"-, 3½"-, and 4½"-wide segments from steps 5 and 6 to make 12 unit C as shown. Combine the fabrics at random. Press the seams however you wish. The units should measure 14½" x 14½" (raw edge to raw edge) when sewn.

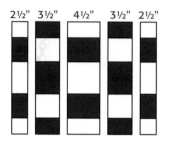
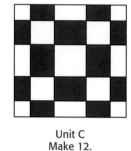

Unit C
Make 12.

Assembling the Quilt Top

1. Join units A, B, and C into rows 1 and 2 as shown. Press the row 1 seams in the opposite direction of the row 2 seams.

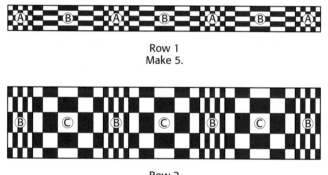

Row 1
Make 5.

Row 2
Make 4.

2. Stitch the rows together as shown. Press the seams in one direction.

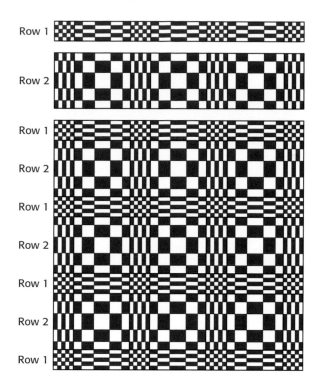

Row 1
Row 2
Row 1
Row 2
Row 1
Row 2
Row 1
Row 2
Row 1

3. Join the inner, middle, and outer borders to the quilt (see "Making Borders with Straight-Cut Corners" on page 18). For the inner border, seam the remaining 2½"-wide green strips as necessary to make strips long enough to border the quilt; press the seams open. Measure the length of the quilt through the center. Cut 2 border strips to the length measured and join them to the sides of the quilt, matching the ends and centers and easing as necessary. Press the seams toward the borders. Measure the width of the quilt through the center, including the border pieces you just added. Cut 2 border strips to the width measured and join them to the top and bottom of the quilt. Press the seams toward the borders. Repeat with the remaining 1½"-wide white-on-white strips for the middle border and the 5½"-wide green strips for the outer border.

Layering and Finishing the Quilt

1. Divide the backing fabric into 3 equal panels. Remove the selvages and join the panels with a ½" seam to make a single, large backing piece. Press the seams open.

2. Center the batting and quilt top on the backing; baste (see "Layering and Basting the Quilt" on pages 21–22).

3. Quilt or tack as desired (see "Quilting" on pages 22–25).

4. Bind the quilt with the remaining 2½"-wide green strips (see "Binding" on pages 26–28).

5. Make a label and stitch it to your quilt (see "Making a Label" on page 28).

ABOUT THE AUTHOR

JUDY HOPKINS is a prolific quilt-maker whose fondness for traditional design goes hand in hand with an unwavering commitment to fast, contemporary cutting and piecing techniques. Judy has been making quilts since 1980 and working full-time at the craft since 1985. Her primary interest is in multiple-fabric quilts; most of her pieces are inspired by classic quilts in a variety of styles. Her work has appeared in numerous exhibits and publications.

Writing and teaching are by-products of Judy's intense involvement in the process of creating quilts. She is author of *One-of-a-Kind Quilts, Fit to Be Tied, Around the Block with Judy Hopkins, Around the Block Again, Down the Rotary Road with Judy Hopkins,* and *Design Your Own Quilts* (a revised and updated version of *One-of-a-Kind Quilts*), and coauthor (with Nancy J. Martin) of *Rotary Riot, Rotary Roundup,* and *101 Fabulous Rotary-Cut Quilts.*

Judy especially enjoys working with scraps. Faced with a daunting accumulation of scraps and limited time to deal with them, she started looking for ways to apply quick cutting methods to scrap fabrics. This led to the design of Judy's popular Scrap-Master ruler, a tool for quick-cutting half-square triangles from irregularly shaped scraps, and the accompanying Blocks and Quilts for the Scrap-Master books.

Judy lives in Juneau, Alaska, with her patient and supportive husband, Bill. She has two grown daughters and four adorable and brilliant grandchildren who like to help her sew.